To order additional copies of this book, contact:

Dr. Kirk Williams
www.drkirkwilliams.com
kirk@drkirkwilliams.com

...I just look like this

A. Kirk Williams M.D.

CONTENTS

• •

INTRODUCTION

• •

We all have our take on the world in which we live. An equation influenced by environment and experiences overlaying a pair of chromosomes, all which represent different variables. So, as you can see the temple or biology that we all live in is not completely our own doing but a set of circumstances that must be navigated. The interesting thing is that regardless how varied the equation, when it comes to our Maker, there is but one correct answer—you are either inside or outside of his wisdom. And nothing we can do as his children can change that. You can't sign a petition, talk loud, or ask someone if it's okay not to obey, or all say at once it's not so, because it is bigger than us all. What is our doing is to recognize and attempt to digest this concept to, in effect, make more wholesome decisions for ourselves and others. No one wakes up and says "I just wanna be this way because I want to," especially when it's wrong. It is, however, a process rooted in teaching, experience, and predisposition based on our genetics, but as in math, it is an equation whose yield is varied based on input. There is a reason for everything, and likewise a process; so let's use this process to yield the right answer, by following the Creator's wishes, and becoming better people, neighbors and stewards of Mother Earth, for our futures, literally, depend on it.

That being said, identifying all the moving parts and connecting all the dots are arduous tasks; maintaining objectivity and mental discipline remains a must. The first step to solving a problem is first admitting there is one. I hope that most people of our era recognize the need for modification of our lifestyles, values, habits, and make adjustments as our moral compasses need refining. We face erosion on many levels but especially spiritual ones, that manifest as mans overextending of his will. He's now playing God and not atoning for his errors but instead rationalizing all the toxic side effects, and pushing forward in his mad pursuit of "Money". Nevermind the caution light that exploded with warnings some time ago. And I'm not simply saying follow all that we have been taught, for there would be no thinning ozone or social or global strife if it were all correct, but it is not.

Through many of my literally works, I attempt to bring these discrepancies and flawed positions to light for examination. To, in effect, assist the unraveling of this web of contrary, self serving, frauds perpetrated against us all, for the benefit of a few. I'm not saying it is exact, for I too am limited in experience, as we all are, but our genes aren't; they have been here since the dawn of man. Instinct and spiritual presence speaks loudly if only you would allow it to, so be quiet and listen. Is it possible to perfect perfection as we rationalize and sanction continued violent, destructive, disobedient behavior—disobedient to our and earth's divineness? And by the way, violent and destructive need not be war, bombings, shootings and murder, but something as simple as ignoring those in need, failing to be our brothers keeper and continued perpetuation of untruths by, allowing man to shape and mold our world with, lies, trinkets and toys, instead of God.

We all think we are getting over, getting by; science disputes this is all but impossible. There is a balance in nature, an equilibrium. Once tipped out of balance, the scales will correct; always, they will correct, as evidenced by wicked weather and conflicts among nations, men and self. So our efforts to threaten, restrict by law, or coerce in any way, the natural reciprocal responses, will fall short, for this is God's will, that abides by His "laws of nature". Not my doing or yours but a cosmic phenomenon that has and will always be. Embrace what is real as set forth by the Creator, for His wisdom is unparalleled, and we really haven't a choice, but just not fully appreciating it yet. As those of less spiritual content will think they are getting away with continued daily cheating of God, acknowledging "how smooth and slick I am", all while spending most of their time paranoid and guilty with their eyes fixed on their review mirrors. As the old cliché goes, the proof is in the pudding. Yes, our actions are responsible for the toxic mental, emotional, spiritual, and physical environments in which we live. Toxic in that there is constant conflict between man's world and God's.

We take instructions given to us by others, i.e., "Society". Others from a group that individually is no different than ourselves, though, obviously less spiritual. We embrace these instructions as if they were scripture, through a process known as socialization, that is really nothing more than plain old fashioned "Brainwashing". This process is not to benefit or serve us but to service those with the power of the pen, as they continue to add zeroes to their net worths, all while ignoring truth, in exchange for fiction. We, on the other hand, are hoodwinked, bamboozled as we remain standing and wondering why our lives are consistently less fulfilled. Embracing the wisdom of God, I suppose, is difficult for those less spiritual, and contagious to those of weakened immunities. Does it take a "Law" to tell you if something is right or wrong, or just because it is a "Law" doesn't determine that it is fair and just, America has too many examples of such. Whatever happened to that internal spiritual compass that has guided our actions since the dawn. Find it, dust it off, and use it in exchange for our pagan worship of the all mighty dollar, remember, as stated "In God we Trust".

Is society as a whole correct when its explained behavior gives way to challenging consequences that literally threatens our own existence? Not seeming to find a breaking point or fully accepting responsibility for these actions because that would mean correction is needed and imminent. Sounds a little bit like a drug addict, doesn't it? Rationalizing to get to what you want at all cost, even acknowledging the possibility yet continuing the hedonistic experience. This is self-imposed as our attention is focused on the small stuff while ignoring the big stuff that will certainly be the demise of us all.

Why do we allow those blatantly irresponsible to continue to pollute our worlds? If their suggestions are inconsistent with and are overall harmful to the ecosystems and well-being that we were all blessed to be born into, then, we must protect it. Take a stand. This is my attempt to do so in a very small way. The lessons of my flesh provides tools to assist in further connecting the dots, as well as, to further interpret this experience we call life, the outcome is what it is. I didn't make the world; I just live in it. In your own small way, have the courage to do the same.

In Memory of My Father, Judge Alphonza Williams

September 10, 1933–September 8, 1997

9-11-2001

As I sit and enjoy the warm September evening breeze, the East Texas September breeze, I remembered as a child at 2207 South Street riding bikes and motorbikes; playing football, basketball, and kickball; shooting marbles—all truly indelible impressions; listening to your favorite tunes, "Take Five" by Dave Brubeck, "It Was a Very Good Year" by Lou Rawls, "My Way" by Frank Sinatra, Bobby "Blue" Bland, B. B. King, Charley Pride; and so on. My heart sheds a tear, for I miss you, though my soul rejoices in your presence and the many, many memories of times with you.

Although it only seems like yesterday, four years have passed since we last spoke. I can hear you now, teaching, caring about me and everyone around you, *giving*, unselfishly sharing wisdom paid for with your life. There is no greater gift, for this truly is the giving of self. I did inherit that heart—thank you. I also inherited that will to be, to do, and to become. You demonstrated an extraordinary commitment to being all you can be. In fact, literally, while on your deathbed, only weeks before your death, I recall your desire to take the bar examination "just one more time." As you so clearly stated and then demonstrated, it is not about the level in life in which you reach; it is, however, about the spirit in which you reach for it. Seldom growing discouraged and always finding a lesson in every experience, pleasant or otherwise, I marvel at your wisdom and strength. I understand it is OK to fail, for failure speaks to—I tried, though; it is never OK not to try again and again and again. Thankfully, this too is a part of me—part genetics, part teaching, and all a blessing from God.

As I sat last evening, counseling my eldest son of four, now an eighth grader, I shared with him one of the many conversations I had with my father when I too was an eighth grader, as though it were yesterday. Thankfully, at least part of it I yielded to; the other part I desperately regret I didn't. It was about being serious about school and becoming a professional. The other was "Son, please don't give up your music for football." Music has always been a true passion for my father and I. Neither of us ever mastered any instrument, only my mother did. "Let me tell you, son, you can't see it now, but when you get older, you're going to wish you continued with your music. I love music and I wish like hell I could blow that horn. Make your own decision. However, if you elect to stop, it will be one of the biggest regrets of your life." Guess what, it is. This conversation mirrored exactly the conversation I had with my son. I smiled and .said to myself, "Daddy, get out of here."

In literature, as in the human saga, multiple themes exist—to name a few, "man vs. man" and "man vs. nature," but as you taught, the most challenging is "man vs. himself." You live life through yourself. Life's biggest struggle is not with others, things, events, etc., but with oneself. Never perfect and fully aware of it, you never hid from me, I respect you for that. You taught "He who conquers himself is the greatest warrior."

I long for September to make way to your gravesite. Resting now next to your mother and father, two people I too love with all my heart, I relax into a visit with my family—I am home. As we recline against a towering oak, beneath the sunset of the beautiful September skies, Little and I both rejoice in memories of times now passed though very alive. Even if only for one moment, we now have you all to ourselves once again. As our visit unfolds, a very familiar yet distant feeling gradually nestles up beside me—a calm, tranquil, soothing feeling that only comes from being at home. For one instant, I am a child again, footloose and fancy-free, playing throughout the neighborhood, embracing times now passed though very alive.

I love you. I miss you. I am proud of you. I remain your pupil.

Your son,

A. Kirk William, MD

The Box

● ●

(7-1-2013)

. . . .Living outside the box, too crowded in, can't see forward for all the skin. . . .

Struggles and Challenges

● ●

(December 10, 2013)

We often credit many of life's struggles and hardships to interference by others, unfortunate circumstances, etc., and although true, we also fail to lay equal blame upon ourselves. Shying away from painful admissions of our own frailties; mentally, emotionally, and spiritually, finding it easier to deflect the truth about ourselves even if not obvious to anyone other than ourselves. Have the courage and pray for the strength to follow the truth wherever it takes you. However, do not be surprised if the truth you seek enters conflict with many of the principles the larger world teaches but in fact confirmation that the truth is real.

No Excuses

• •

(December 10, 2013)

When challenged regarding our way of thinking—slanted, jaded, and obviously misguided—our response is "But this is how I was raised" or "This is what my parents taught"—doesn't matter. We are living centuries of misguidance; the only equalizer is truth. Connect the dots as they are all around you, but our conditioning is so perfected we won't even drink from the fresh spring of truth.

Nobody Has Quite Figured This Out Yet

• •

(January 6, 2014)

With the current of society running in one direction, the current in your heart running in another direction, and the current of your mind running, yet still in another direction, all free-flowing, independent, and with its own agenda; everyone needs to proceed with caution. Never considering, for purposes of health and well-being, that all share the same rail space, your mind, body, and soul. It's obvious that the closed system of railing with its many intersections will eventually give way to collisions of varying consequence if not piloted in an orderly fashion. Who's ticketed or who's at fault is a question deferred to the Maker as he assigns the right-of-way, having engineered all the technical aspects of this elaborate system of rails, he is best suited. Its Maker likewise is most suited to suggest the rules of operation—when to stop, how fast in the curves and straightaways, required stopping distances, how many passengers per car, required maintenance, and so on.

With all processes running simultaneously and competing for resources, attention, and preference, it's nearly impossible to make sense of it all. Prioritizing and following the rules enables smooth operation

of this magical machine. Without the heart, nothing is possible, for within it lies all the spoken truths from God and rightfully so demands the yield from all, the right-of-way, if I may. Without heeding to the rules, it's not *if* but *when* the inevitable collisions will occur, which we experience in our daily lives as they manifest themselves as anxiety, confusion, depression, stress, alcoholism, drug addiction, loneliness, isolation, financial failure, substandard job performance, divorce, low self-esteem, insecurity, homicide, suicide, and thinning ozone, as—the descriptions continue. The current of society is akin to the current in your mind. However, neither is akin to the current in your heart. If the currents of mind and society were healthy and consistent with the heart, the conflict of body, mind, and soul's net yield would be all but nebulous. You see, when you are unaware of certain principles and haven't tasted certain ingredients as the chef, there is no way to include them in your mix. For example, after midday meals, Mexicans of Mexico have siestas. Why? Because it's consistent with the way we are made; this reflects the current in our heart. Our response to this scenario by US standards or standards rooted in capitalism is that this decreases productivity. However, if properly studied and with slight modification to the rigid, cold, heartless models used, it probably isn't, but that's another story. This example, however simple, all but illustrates one of the many principles of separation of mind and heart or stated in a more recognizable way by the old cliché "the separation of mind and body." As suggested above, God made us a certain way, and by staying within ourselves and within his wisdom mentally, emotionally, and spiritually, we can achieve happiness and health on all levels..

In light of the problems challenging our society and its people, if somehow more would take heed, self-correction and restoration would prevail. Though this is but a pipe dream because the authors of our society, having set the wheel in motion many moons ago, themselves lived outside of this understanding, some a fault of their own, others not, as their physiology would not permit. So think of yourself as different because somehow including them and their thought processes as your own only serves to confuse one further (the distinctions of which will be discussed in a separate article). Nevertheless, the antidote is to dissect ourselves in an effort to understand who we are and whose we are. I'm not talking about the obvious, as I can hear the disgruntled sighs from here, to suggest that "I don't know who I am." I understand that fully, but I'm talking about using an objective search tool outside of what we already know, because obviously, the one we've been using is biased and hasn't worked. Likened to the surrender of the compass in the earth's magnetic field, pure, unadulterated, consistent, timeless, and true only to the truth.

You very well cannot solve a problem or even identify one using the very same instruments and tools employed to create them (i.e., this is defined as "in the box"). Speaking and thinking the language and following the rules the system teaches as it benefits only itself, in perpetuity, never mind that it lies far outside of the wisdom of God, fully embracing this system, never questioning it as if it were created out of divineness that mirrors ours, though it is not, for this is but cosmic slop.

Let's take an imaginary journey back to our birth. Moving forward in life, several dynamics are in play—to name a few, absorption of the spoken language, social values, taste for certain foods, and so on—often long before even a spoken word. Shortly thereafter, while still young and extremely impressionable, formal education occurs and all that it entails. Many years will have passed before any notions of established foundations as a basis for our bias is recognized. All of which stems from decades and even centuries of defenseless absorption of the environment, or quite simply, assimilation. Over time, we are fed whatever's on the table. Now, that's all we have an appetite for, wielding it as our own free will, most having any idea that no, it's not—it is simply conditioning, which is of man, not God.

By the time we are of age to recognize or have even a remote look into this process, we've already taken the bait and never looked back, digesting and representing the absorbed, assimilated standards as our own, the ultimate form of mind control, or restated another way, brainwashing at its absolute best. Now, however, the task before us, arduous and complex as these standards represent our foundations in life, and hence any unfavorable comments viewed as personal attacks but actually it is not, just an attempt to unravel. So most will wrestle and fight these concepts to no end, not because they are untrue but because they are perceived as personal attacks on the foundation of their lives, that happens to be the assimilated ground beneath their feet. Many have fought and struggled most of their lives to find what they consider that sweet spot , through rationalization, prayer, denunciation of alternative ideas, etc. But having described this process alone supports the author's position. Does it make sense that God created the universe and all its children so that daily struggle for peace and happiness is commonplace? No, it doesn't for good reason because it's not His doing; if so, it would flow and compliment our nature that is his. Instead, it antagonizes on all levels—mentally, emotionally, spiritually, financially, physically, and so on. When a machine is working optimally, it performs its assigned tasks optimally and not the opposite, for that is a sign something is wrong.

Consider this for example. If you think and are proud of the fact that you exercise free will in your life's decisions, think with me through this process. Is it truly free will if the dinner selections served are one of four as you choose one of them? Or one step further, are you truly independent in your exercising of free will as all four selections offered to choose from were chosen for you, again, "in the box," not out? I have noted over time that the arguments for or against our progressive and accomplished society are done so by using the very standards set by society itself. How can this be objective, measuring a system against itself and not by outside standards? Yes, it's all difficult to unravel because we know nothing else. We speak and live only within the confines of the alphabet, which represents yet another box to climb out of. It's diabolical in fact but had to be to reach and maintain control of the planet for some two thousand years. First, digesting the concept of containment within the box is but one thing; then, followed by, an attempt to unravel this social web of bondage on multiple layers is but another. Quite frankly, though, by design, most will find it virtually impossible to muster enough energy to fight more self-directed battles in search of peace as much energy has already been expended in this process and can be quite painstaking as it is, however, the foundation of our lives.

We all are prejudiced. We like what we have been taught to like and dislike what we have been taught to dislike, not all our own doing but merely absorption of our environment on all levels. A very simple question that requires complex self-analysis is, How much of you is you, and how much of you is purely the regurgitation of your environment? Where do you draw the line, or are you even aware there is a line, or have you drank so much of the poison that you are unaware and drunken?

Most are looking for quick one-sentence answers that will magically change their position in life, granting them eternal happiness by the standards of the assimilated world, or a yes-no question. Sorry to disappoint you, but it ain't happening. All the Band-Aids are no more. Dig down deep and attempt to undo what's been done to you. Regurgitate as much as possible your notions of superiority or inferiority because they don't exist as God's standards, only as man's. So what if you've designed the model T and flight (that's now a booming industry by these standards and has erected massive buildings or created material wealth). In short, do not use the self-professed standards as set forth by the industrial revolution as evidence of progress, for it is certainly not factual or consistent with the natural laws of nature but, in fact, to it's detriment, so does that yield by definition it a root of good or a root of evil? This system is but a reflection of its authors; it did not make itself.

So we find ourselves in a vicious cycle, bending our knees in prayer for strength from the one system, to be used in the system where we live, which, as outlined, is corrosive to the system that we pray to—go figure. And "No One has Quite Figured this Out Yet" or certainly not acknowledged it. Man's desires now supersede his Maker's, and yet he expects continued support and favor. This is but an impossibility. If it were possible to treat as an equation in math, it would be considered to be incongruent—it doesn't match, the wrong answer. Man has been on the planet 6 million years, plus-minus a few, to the best of our knowledge, and seemingly shared the planet and resources equitably. Of course, in the beginning man as we define him was of a different nature, newly welcomed to the earth scene by his Maker and eternally grateful as he remained a good steward of the planet, until recent times. Prior to, human practices, behavior, and attitudes regarding Mother Earth were that of a harmonious nature; now quite the opposite, which leaves one to ask the question, where is all this headed? Because we live here day to day and witness only gradual changes; we fail to fully appreciate the rapidity of change. Likened to raising a child and not fully aware of his or her growth as your eyes are tuned in daily only to be surprised by Grandma's observation as she makes her yearly visit—"Wow, that kid has really grown."

History will view us and these times the same. Things are occurring at warp speed, and we are asleep at the wheel. In our arrogance and self-professing progressiveness, are our accomplishments truly greater and superior to the generations and eras that preceded us? Before, they were blessed by our Maker and stayed within bounds of his wisdom. Primitive, as we refer to them. However, their law-abiding practices were at peace and harmony with nature. I wonder what they would say about us. Now you answer the question, although I know we may not all be church people, but most are certainly spiritual and all claim to place God first. How then do you reconcile the sign of these times?

Common Denominator

(2008)

In all the complexities of life, notwithstanding all the psychological warfare that we all have been victims of, knowingly and unknowingly, we all have sustained injury, some active and others healed, that we wear as scars. How much of you is you, and how much of you is purely the regurgitation of your environment? "Coke," is it? Got to have a pair of Air Jordans? Who are you, and where do you exist? What defines the being that you are, and where is that being nourished? That is a contemporary question that reflects the value system of the society in which we are socialized, and that does change. One hundred years ago, it was one thing; six hundred years ago, it was something else; today, something else; so on and so forth. But one thing we know for sure is that the heartbeat of man has never changed. The core being that defines us has been consistent since the dawn of time. Embrace contemporary thought as it changes, minute by minute, and yields persistent insecurity as a by-product, or embrace that core being that has lived within you since the dawn of man. For that is the being that was kissed by the Creator and given a to-do list. Sure, value systems change daily and even by the minute; however, embracing God, the common denominator, consistently yields peace.

ANXIETY

• •

(2008)

The human condition keeps us all in the box, wondering, thinking about the future, looking for peace and security, which tend to be fleeting. Mainly because our minds are telling us one thing; television, news media, catalogues of attractive people, etc., and our hearts our God-given gifts are telling us something else. Mind in one place heart in another creates a delta; that gulf is defined as anxiety. As mind and body approach one, so does the calm and tranquility we define as peace. People will live their entire lives and die in pursuit of what's supposed to be important about life, never really knowing what really is important about life, looking to complexities in the social, mental, emotional, and spiritual realms for the answer.

There is nothing complex about life; it is simple, beautiful, and a blessing. It is our weaknesses, lack of courage, and lack of understanding of God's wisdom that will not allow us to stare life in its face and see it for what it is. Rather we want to see it for what we want it to be. Dealing with it for what it is may require something of us, like getting out of our comfort zones or maybe even admitting that we have been wrong or maybe even changing our ways. All this "supposed to be" stuff is just that—stuff. What is, is for a reason. Our Maker has already defined the order to the universe, which includes everything imagined and otherwise. Nothing is new but rather just not recognized or perceived. If as you peer through the windows of cognition and encounter impediments to your view by way of smears, stains, or even fractures, so then is your perspective. Proper spiritual hygiene and maintenance will assist you with a clearer vision.

It Is What It Is

• •

(2008)

When debating and attempting to rationalize human behavior, let's first start with some truths, not just assume that everyone is created equal because that is politically correct. How can you very well examine truthfully the chemical, emotional, and spiritual elements that have brought us to this day without crossing the lines of political correctness or certainly encroaching on personal opinions, founded and unfounded, to in effect determine the affirmative? Pierce the veil of personal and political correctness and incorporate an ancient philosophical thought process known as logic. The powers to be have gotten completely away from the truth as is yielded by simple logic. For example, if you throw a rock up, it comes down. This principle has existed since the beginning of time. We can gather around the round table and debate this phenomenon indefinitely, and when we are done, it is what it is. Why should it be anything other than what it is? This phenomenon reflects the laws of nature in its purest form. Rather it should be embraced as something set forth by our Maker that is pure, unadulterated truth. Mentally, emotionally, and spiritually, these same principles exist. Since the time in which the first woman and man appeared on the planet, the Creator had already spoken. The laws of nature that govern behavior, understanding, relationships, and the capacity to love, learn, and teach were already perfected; it remains our duty to find it.

DREADS

• •

(January 14, 2014)

Imitation of Life is a late 1950s movie that deals with race, where a black lady gives birth to a little girl fathered by a white man, in which the child inherited her father's very fair skin. However, unbeknownst to her mother when away from home, the daughter, while denying her black heritage, was passing for white. Also, throughout her life, the daughter would avoid public affection and appearances with her mother for fear of exposure as to her true ethnicity. The movie did spotlight, however, among other things, the backlash of sentiment experienced once the daughter's true ethnicity was known.

My family's bloodline has but a similar intersection, in which my mother, Laura Veazey Williams, in her book *Born and Not Wanted*, celebrates the life and times of her mother, Laura Elizabeth Kuykendall Veazey, where similar crossings of paths occurred between a wealthy rancher's son, Isaac Kuykendall, and his African cook's daughter, Minnie Allanise, nine months prior to November 1895, yielding a beautiful mulatto baby girl.

The Kuykendall bloodline places us on horseback with the father of Texas, Stephen F. Austin, as he crossed the Colorado River into Texas in 1820. At this crossing was one family camped on the Texas side of the bank, awaiting their arrival, as four families traveled with him, three of which were Kuykendalls—Abner, Joseph, and Robert H., whom our brand is a direct descendant of, for this caravan represented the very first Texans. This is the same Texas history that my boys recalled studying as eighth graders as they where doubted by their teachers and classmates alike after revealing their descent. What a hell of a story for a twelve—or thirteen-year-old to make up. Oh well. In many circles, Robert H. is credited as the father of the famed Texas Rangers. The early settlers were plagued by Indian warfare, the Karankawas. Robert H. developed a successful system to combat them. This was in the early 1820s. The Rangers didn't come into existence until the mid-1830s. He was dead by now as he had suffered a head injury during battle, requiring a trepan (burr hole), after which he was never the same and died a year or two later. His legacy, however, lived on. It takes reading the print from the authors of the day to describe his superior abilities and skills on horseback. All that's missing is the cape, for he was a true warrior. Nevertheless, the Indian defense model developed by Captain Robert Hardin Kuykendall was adopted by the Ranger bunch and thus credited him as father of the famed Texas Rangers.

It is my grandmother Laura Elizabeth Kuykendall Veazey's Pierce bloodline that reaches back to the founding fathers of this country as they sailed west to the New World over the cold, choppy Atlantic waters on the *Mayflower* in 1620. I'm not sure how much everyone remembers about this story.

The *Mayflower* voyage initially set out for the colony of Virginia in September 1620 in an attempt to escape religious persecution from King James and the Church of England but, as a result of stormy weather, was forced to drop anchor on the western shore of the hook of Cape Cod, Massachusetts, near present-day Provincetown, Massachusetts, on November 11, 1620. It was at this time even before stepping foot onto American soil on November 13, 1620, that a social document was created, designed to prevent dissent among Puritans and nonseparatist Pilgrims and signed by forty-one male *Mayflower* passengers, two of which we are direct descendants, called the *Mayflower* compact. This was the first written framework of government established in what is now the United States and credited as the foundation for the United States Constitution. After unsuccessfully scouting for three weeks for a suitable location to establish a settlement, the Pilgrims set sail north for Plymouth Harbor, arriving at Plymouth Rock, Massachusetts, on December 16, 1620. The first winter proved extremely challenging as the one hundred and two *Mayflower* passengers dwindled to fifty-two as a result of poor nutrition and inadequate housing. Squanto, as the legend is told, taught the Pilgrims how to grow corn and where to fish and trap beavers and as a consequence all but ensured their survival in the New World, and the rest, as they say, is history. These are the blessings we celebrate every November known as Thanksgiving.

Nevertheless, as the one-percent rule goes which, by the way, applies only to one race in the United States, as established by the wishes of God, Thomas Jefferson, I, as well as, all my family members have lived our entire lives proudly as black Americans, and sure many could, as we say in the south, have passed.

Through Grandmother Susan Head Pierce Kuykendall's bloodline, we are direct descendants of the *Mayflower* passengers John Alden and Priscilla Mullins as well as Priscilla's parents, William and Alice Mullins. The lineage looks something like this: My sons, Anthony Kirk Williams II, Austin Kyle Williams, Alexander Kuykendall Williams and Adam Kristopher Williams-Anthony Kirk Williams MD-Laura Veazey Williams-Laura Elizabeth Kuykendall Veazey-Isaac Kuykendall-Susan Head Pierce Kuykendall (sister to Abel Head "Shanghai" Pierce)-Hannah Head Pierce (mother to Abel Head "Shanghi" Pierce)-Daniel-Ruth Little-Fobes-Martha Pabodie-Elizabeth Alden-John Alden/Priscilla Mullins-William/Alice Mullins. We have four documented forefathers and one uncle, Priscilla's brother Joseph, that were *Mayflower* passengers first stepping onto this American soil at Cape Cod and Plymouth, Massachusetts, in the year of our Lord 1620.

Famous cousins of direct lineage, to name a few, include the second president and the first vice president of the United States, John Adams; the sixth president of the United States, John Quincy Adams; the fourteenth president of the United States, Franklin Pierce; the United States vice president under President Herbert Walker Bush, James Danforth Quayle; Norma Jeane Baker, better known as Marilyn Monroe; world-renown chemist and founder of Dow Chemical, Herbert Henry Dow; world-renown poet Henry Wadsworth Longfellow (as his poem "The Courtship of Miles Standish" earned him national acclaim); George Orson Welles, considered to be one of the greatest directors not only of film but also of theater; and Abel Head "Shanghai" Pierce, Texas cattle baron that owned and operated over 250,000 acres, the second-largest ranch in Texas, second only to the King Ranch at the time of his death in December 1900. He also imported Brahma cattle from India which furnished Texas and subsequently the United States with base stock from which large herds of Brahmas have grown (he was my grandmother's great-uncle) and my grandmother's first cousin, which also doubled as her best friend her entire life was Winnie Phillips whose husband, Hokie Phillips, was the original founder of Phillips 66 oil and gas company. Other cousins once removed, as all the surviving fifty-two *Mayflower* passengers' bloodlines are intermingled at some point, include the twelfth president of the United States, Zachary Taylor; the eighteenth president of the United States, Ulysses Grant; the twentieth president of the United States, James Garfield; the thirty-second president of the United States, Franklin Delano Roosevelt; the thirty-seventh president of the United States, Richard Nixon; the thirty-eighth president of the United States, Gerald Ford; the forty-first president of the United States, George Herbert Walker Bush; the forty-third president of the United States, George Walker Bush; Sir Winston Churchill; Ralph Waldo Emerson; Henry David Thoreau; Noah Webster (as in the dictionary); poet William Cullen Bryant; Mormon founder and leader, Joseph Smith; Humphrey Bogart; Bing Crosby; Johnny Carson; Hugh Hefner; Clint Eastwood; Christopher Reeve; Alan B Shepard; Richard Gere; the Baldwin brothers; the Beach Boys; and Dick Van Dyke—to name, I would say a few, but to name more than a few, as this list continues.

Though all our lives we have lived completely outside of this fanfare, as some family members are still unaware, nevertheless, Grandmother always proudly made references to her lineage but forbade public acknowledgment of such for fear of embarrassing her grandparents. Even though she was raised by her grandparents in the big house as a wealthy white girl, she never knew her African heritage until told by a field hand at the age of fourteen or fifteen as she asked him to saddle a horse for her evening ride. His reply was "You do it yourself, you're as black as I am." Upon hearing of such, as rumor has it, Grandpa Wylie Martin Kuykendall gathered up his shotgun with a handful of shotgun shells and left that field hand right where he found him. I know it doesn't make sense to us now. However, life during the turn of the century for people of color smelled of sweat from a long day's work in the fields for mere crumbs, while the landscape was sprinkled with nooses around black necks hanging from trees as a means to continue instilling fear. All while the US government turned a blind eye. People of color had very, very few options. Her thanks and gratitude was for the lifelong generosity and kindness of her grandparents as they never threw her away but, in fact, did quite the opposite. Flashes of the same brilliance, however, did express itself throughout her gene pool of eleven children and their offspring as well. Although blessed with many of the same gifts and talents, race, however, did serve as a wedge. Nevertheless, we never missed what we never had. Still the celebrations have been numerous and equaled with much love to match.

I am myself a light-skinned black American that inherited my mother's color, which is, as we say in the south, light bright and damn near white. In retrospect, I may have spoken too soon regarding my family members not passing for white. I can, however, recall many stories of my mother's fairness, but there is one I would like to share that clearly falls into the category of passing and for good reason. I was born in Marshall, Texas, in December 1959, approximately two hundred miles from my mom's hometown, Dickinson, Texas, midway between Houston and Galveston. At least two to three times a year, my family would make that trip to visit the extended family, usually during Christmas and July 4, my grandfather's birthday. This incident occurred during her third trimester of pregnancy with me while traveling the long, narrow road from Marshall to Dickinson. As with most pregnant mothers, having babies lying and kicking on their bladders all day, she had to pee. During those days, there were very few accommodations for coloreds to use restrooms, purchase gas for their cars, or even buy food

for their kids while traveling. Nevertheless, running out of time, they decided to pull into the next gas station regardless. The attendant immediately made it clear they were welcome only for gas. So after gassing up, my father pulled out and back around, parking on the side of the station, letting my mom out to go into this full store and do her business. Not even a brow was wrinkled. Stories like these, unfortunately, are beyond numerous.

Nevertheless, years ago I considered myself clean-cut and preppy. Later, however, after closing a fairly substantial real estate deal while simultaneously experiencing the midlife "crazies," I chose to experiment with a youthful look. I followed one of my buddies' leads, also a doctor, into deciding to grow my hair out into dreadlocks. This was ballsy from where I set, small-town America in southeast Texas, some twenty miles from a known Ku Klux Klan hub and seventy miles from where James Byrd Jr. was drugged to death. Nevertheless, I was still the same person, Dr. Williams, just with a different "do" that celebrated my blackness as many of the ancient cultures, including the Egyptians so did. Offensive as it must have been, that I still don't understand, though not intentional, it only served as an expression of self—not good enough for you but good enough for *God*. If I were not supposed to have these naps, I wouldn't. I met it with a silent resistance, which only served to further strengthen my commitment to continue. I recall thinking many times how my fair skin, coupled with other features, may have played a role before as apparently my true nationality was not known, or certainly I was not readily labeled as black, or if I was, it was qualified by statements like "But you're not the same." Now, however, without a doubt, dreads undeniably revealed my true DNA as I screamed in celebration of my ethnicity. I have always been proud of my heritage while embracing my ancestors on both sides. As the cliché states, you are a product of your past experiences, and if you are proud of yourself, then you alternatively are also proud of the ingredients.

However, my kinship obviously is far more consistent with that of the African than otherwise, as Thomas Jefferson made that call many moons ago. As a result of that four-hundred-year period in American history known as slavery, blacks' birth and death records were not maintained, only as far as it related to their owners' balance sheets. I learned this firsthand while trying to retrieve my grandmother's birth certificate at the Matagorda County courthouse some years back, and she was considered privileged. The county didn't start recording these records for blacks until the turn of the century. I guess, in all fairness, why keep records of such, for slaves were not people with souls, only chattel, no different than a chair or horse. Slaves were totally at the mercy of their massa's whims as he can do as he pleases with their bag of bones, up to and including disposing of them at will, while suffering absolutely no consequence. So tracing your black heritage proves to be difficult, for if you have any success at all, it usually dead-ends into slavery.

I have traced my father's bloodline six generations back to Jack standing alone in an 1850s Mississippi cotton field; nothing else is known. I am equally proud of him for he especially was a soldier—brave, strong, and alone. This is all but typical of American black lineage, which is probably the richest of all as it dates back to the dawn of man. All too often I dissect my makeup in an attempt to understand where different character traits are rooted. I know to most this doesn't make sense, though you haven't been where I have. The artistic abilities—creativity, writing, architectural design, music, etc.—as well as math and science skills clearly reflect the bunch above. But determination, courage, hope, and strength, I credit the African Jack, for he has had much to overcome. I know him well as he lives within me and lived within my father before me and his father before him and so on. But there was no greater example of Jack's determination and desire to succeed than exhibited by his son Alphonza Williams, my father. He was born a "twin" in 1933 small-town America, on the other side of the tracks, to uneducated, hardworking parents that wielded a superior moral compass. He always had a dream of becoming a professional as I was pounded with this concept my entire life—not doctor or lawyer, but professional. He was never given a chance to succeed.

He joined the Marshall Police Department with Jean Whitaker in 1958 as the two first black policemen ever in the history of East Texas. This proved to be a very challenging time in his life, so much so that upon my birth in 1959, he refused to name me Junior for fear of retaliation if he were forced to harm someone in his line of work. The stories and challenges were numerous. For example, he was not allowed to arrest white citizens his first four years on the police force, which speaks volumes. Writing tickets or accosting someone white was prohibited. He would have to call for white backup officers and the closest would respond to carry on. Or while on duty and in uniform, he literally had the keys to the city. However, in civilian clothes, there were downtown stores he could not frequent. Woolworth, for example, would suddenly have a severe case of amnesia and dismiss all the good deeds he performed—from returning stolen items retrieved from shoplifters to accosting would-be intruders wearing masks. The order of the day somehow managed to prevail. Also, all too often when white officers were in pursuit of someone black, racial epitaphs would spill over the airway on their closed-circuit police radios: "Get that nigger." "Got me a nigger." "Where did that nigger go?" This would happen over and over again and infuriate him to no end. However, he would let it be known. The police chief at that time shared a great deal of affection for my father. He recognized the challenges he faced and admired how he handled such indignities with such dignity. Many of the officers that committed these offenses initially refused to apologize. However, over time and with such increasing respect for my father, there came a time when those same officers would rather shoot themselves in the foot than stand or allow anyone else to stand on the foot of Alphonza Williams.

He ultimately graduated through the ranks to serve as the first black sergeant and detective before leaving the police force to attend law school in 1973, returning to become the first black judge in East Texas. Since his death, the Marshall Police and Fire Department complex was named in his honor, representing one of the few municipal buildings in this country named after a black American.

Probably the most challenging times as a police officer occurred in the mid 1960s. The national civil rights movement was in full swing, and Marshall was the proud home of two black colleges: Bishop College and my parents' alma mater, Wiley College, as well as a white college, East Texas Baptist College. My father was torn between the two worlds: how to separate the human from the human experience, recognizing the obvious need for change versus the sworn oath and commitment to uphold the law. Many times he would return to the city jail with his patrol car full of protesting college students. I later learned he had many talks with the arrested students while handcuffed and riding in the backseat of his patrol car, and his message was clear: "You guys are doing the right thing, keep doing what you are doing. I'm just doing my job but just keep doing what you are doing. Change has to come. I do applaud your efforts." To this day, many of those accounts have come full circle, grown legs and arms right there before me, and spoken loudly about those experiences and how it shaped and molded their approach to conflict in their lives since those days forward.

Up until the day he died, he never crossed paths with a stranger regardless of their background. These examples provide some insight into the temperament of a man facing daily inequities as he remained balanced, respectful, and positive—sounds a lot like Jack to me.

Today, however, something as simple as a hairdo precipitates what I loosely define as alternative treatment but really reflects rude, disrespectful behavior. Now as I enter a store, seeking an item requiring assistance, it comes as brash, rushed, and bothered—or the gas attendant that purposefully would call those white behind me in line "Next"; or the new bankers not yet familiar with me, shifting eyes as I enter to deposit my lucky wad of winnings from my recent casino trip; or the flight attendant that sent me to the back of the plane, separated from the group I was traveling with on a full return flight from Salt Lake City, as he made accommodations for the others, even threatening to block my flight altogether and call security if I didn't stop my protest at once; or the hospital's election to terminate a profitable contract I held for over ten-plus years without discretion for the preference of outsiders that brought nothing to the table but their skin—all of which are now the past.

However, ongoing, as I am still a practicing emergency physician, the new patient encounters remain interesting. For those uncomfortable, you can pretty much palpate their anxiety. Others, however, could care less and are very appreciative of good care. Nevertheless, your professionalism must be heightened with explanations and flashes of brilliance to allay fears of incompetence, which is expected. My impulse is to explain it's not what's on your head but what's in your head. The surface matters not. In short, massive compensation for the appearance of who you are is still met with resistance and unsteadiness. My condition can change easily with a pair of borrowed clippers. Others, however, that more closely resemble the African, "the original man," I can only imagine.

Many people of color are often labeled as having a chip on their shoulders, having lived somewhat on both sides of the equation, though not completely, but close enough for insight. I have witnessed discrimination in its rarest and most complex forms, so refined, gracious, and smooth that, were the African not alert within me , could easily have been missed. Accomplished in my own right, and now, as outlined above, even with a pedigree that smells of American royalty, I still have to face checkmates with most new public encounters. How ironic as we minimize the impact of race in America—I don't think so. Nevertheless, I still face the next encounter with a determined eagerness, for within me is a repertoire of accomplishment that if pushed will silence most—no, don't go there.

Sunday morning is filled with pews of those wanting to be like Jesus though never missing an opportunity to weasel out once the opportunity presents. You see, we all have our crosses to bear. I am just blessed to be able to share this one with my Maker, for he looks like me.

Aunt Minnie

• •

This is my aunt, a wife, mother, daughter, sister and friend. Someone I have known and loved all of my life. When asked to stand and make some comments at a time like this my first response was I would love to but because of the closeness, I don't know if I can. Memories of her take me literally back to some of the first smiles I remember as a child; Then I was quickly reminded, depending on the author "Oh no this is what Minnie," if you are talking to Uncle Louis, "Oh no, this Is what mother", if you are talking to Alfreda or Louella, or "Oh, no, this is what your aunt Minnie", wanted, if talking to my mom. It was completely evident, very quickly I DIDN'T EVEN MUCH have a choice. This small and benign exchange however, speaks volumes about the love, respect, and admiration that everyone has for this lady. As the old saying goes, "an apple doesn't fall too far from the tree", Is never more evident than in the life of MINNIE, after her mother's mother, ESTELL, after her father's mother, VEAZEY GILL. Loving caring, fair, unselfish, God fearing, peace maker, determined to do the right thing like her mother Laura Elizabeth Kuykendall, Coupled with the strength, and stubbornness of her father George Joseph Veazey. This translates into "If you don't want to Know don't even ask." She would not lie to you or for you –period, and love you just the same. And don't come back later thinking you can present the same scenario a different way and get a buy in "ain't gonna happen." Who you are or who you think you are won't change a thing.

From the mind and heart of a child, 1904 sunset drive was a special place. Driving into Dickinson on two laned I-45, in the mid to late 60's seemed to take forever to get from the south side of Houston, especially when you are an only child; eager with anticipation of seeing all your many cousins, aunts, uncles and grandparents. For me, it just didn't get any better than this. But a pattern of behavior began back then for me that continues to this day. 'Whenever I drive into Dickinson one of my first stops is almost always at Aunt Minnie's and Uncle Louis's. When I was finally old enough to remember and follow Directions any variation that didn't take us straight to 1904 Sunset Drive, would create, should I say, "conflict in our vehicle." Upon arrival, if Uncle Louis wasn't working, he would always be the first person you would see in the yard. Always busy doing something. Cutting grass, feeding and watering the cows, building or repairing the fence, it really didn't matter, but he was always busy doing something. The second thing you couldn't miss was a little bare footed and I underline barefoot, all the time, curly headed little fellow either tagging along behind his dad or riding Shabo the terror, miniature pony. But it really didn't matter to little Louis because if Shabo wasn't available, he would simply ride King, the resident German Shepard in the front yard. All of this is happening long before you get inside where Aunt Minnie would have all the girls busy cooking, cleaning or just simply straightening up and this occurred on a daily basis. This you still see today. If you ever eat at her house or even at your own house with any of her girls, if you are not careful before you are done eating, they

will almost be done cleaning the kitchen, putting away all left overs and looking for something else to help with. Now Barbara, being the baby girl obviously took very good notes because she takes cleaning and straightening up to a completely different level. You will be left thinking, now how did she know how to do it like that. The girls were always happy to see us too, because visiting family members was one of the few excused detours from house work.

Visits around Christmas were always special. The house would be filled with all of the sights and fresh aromas of the holiday season. But my favorite was when we would all gather around the piano to sing Christmas Carols. Boy, Between Debra, Louella, Auntie, my mom and Uncle Louis on bass, you couldn't believe your ears. It truly was something to hear. However, back in the day I do remember thinking to myself onetime "I'm thinking little Louis has the better end of this deal.". And being little boys of course, we were always mischievous. The older girls would threaten to beat us within an inch of our lives. But we already had a solution. As long as auntie was within running distance, we were in good shape. She already knew we deserved to get out butts beat but no, no, not her boys. You already know little Louis being the youngest in the house, as well as the only boy, momma, daddy and big sisters all had him rotten. So Auntie, being a little sister and now a big sister, wife and mother of 7, had already sharpened her skills on how to extend her love to spoil the rest of us. And she did a good job of it. In fact, it just continued into the next generation of hard heads, Little Moses, Sylvester Jr., Michael, Jay Michael, Chris and Devin. This list also includes granddaughters and greats—La Tasha, Kia, Ann, Chloe, Brittany, Mariah, Ashley and Terry. But notice I left Terry, better known as, Tinky Lynn for last because I couldn't convince myself she didn't deserve to be in a class all of her own. This list also includes her only daughter-In-law, Carla, son-In-laws past and present, nieces and nephews. She had all of our respect. But when we were kids she also had a secret weapon that we respectfully referred to as "THE BELT" or "THE PAINT STICK" And she could use it well with either hand.

You know auntie was also the family doctor, house calls and all. I remember times throughout the years when any one of the 30 plus first cousins would get injured while playing during July 4th on the big lawn while celebrating Granddaddy's Birthday and everyone would be freaking out, especially Ella B, who still today would pass out at the sight of blood Auntie would say "now come here and let me take a look at it," tell you exactly what to do to fix it with not even an increase In her blood pressure, turn and go right back to what she was doing as if nothing ever happened. And certainly, over the years, sisters and brothers, mother and father, nieces and nephews, and of course, Uncle Louis and her own children when faced with health concerns would always seek her input first. Minnie, do you think it could be this, or momma could it be that"? The old man himself took his last breath with his head on her lap and aunt Winnie's arms. Right before her illness was confirmed I recall a conversation between the two of us where she basically admitted the reason she was not in a hurry to get diagnosed because she already knew there was a problem. "That's why I kept putting off my work-up until l returned from my European trip. But everything is going to be alright, I've lived a good clean and healthy life and God has blessed me with a wonderful family. So if this is God's will then SO BE IT". And you can hear her saying that even right now. I further remember times after I had finished medical school and was a practicing physician, I'd catch myself in discussions with Auntie as if I was speaking to another physician, and she didn't miss a beat. Her love of science is best expressed through her two daughters, Janice and Debra, a Biologist and a Chemist respectfully.

Last but not least, you know grandmother left behind many legacies, one of which is a great topic of discussion in this family, COOKING. Because you know all of her children, let them tell it, can cook, the girls and the boys. Listening to Frank Fredrick Veazey, pontificate, "I'm the greatest cook in the world, momma taught me everything." Of course, I couldn't wait to tell Colquitt what Fredrick said because I knew exactly what was about to happen. Ever heard of "The Great Debaters?" It was on. The truth is either one of them could make you hurt yourself. Now Jess, on the other hand, never claimed to be the greatest cook in the world, but he is the best eater in the world. And he is gonna do that 2-3 times a day, every day, come rain or high water and if he chooses to cook every day, which he has no problem doing, you cannot convince him it's not gourmet. Now Uncle Robert pretty much knew Aunt Margie had this area under control and "got dang, got dang" he wasn't going to mess with it. Everybody pretty much knows Uncle Louis's barbeque is legendary. The smell of the grill and the taste of the 4th is practically a family trademark. I recall just 2-3 weeks ago Audrey was trying to figure out how to get her dad to barbeque because all she wanted was "some of my daddy's 'Texas Barbeque'". Now the girls on the other hand are pretty straight forward. You can tell who the good cooks are, just by listening. The ones that never talk about how good that meal was they just prepared are the ones. I think that would be Aunt Minnie and Aunt Winnie. Being politically correct as she was all of her life, I can hear her saying right now, "now Kirk don't you start nothing up in here or I'll get that paint stick after you." But one thing is for certain, it is and was a WHOLE LOT OF FUN sitting amongst my aunts and uncles over the years and just taking it all in. There is one area of distinction that clearly belongs to auntie. Grandmother started a family tradition that on special occasions such as birthdays, holidays and anniversaries, she would prepare the infamous LADY BALTIMORE CAKE. With grandmothers passing, Minnie was the only one left that could authenticate this recipe. So much so, that if you even mentioned THE Lady Baltimore Cake around Colquitt, he would have a visible reaction. His last Christmas with us, short of breath and all, Brother was awakened by his dad getting up, dressed, and on his way out the door. When asked where he was going, he simply replied, "Minnie made me a Lady Baltimore Cake for Christmas and I'm on my way to get it." The fact that – By this time he couldn't even drive – hadn't even registered. So I think it's safe to say that even "The Great Debaters" knew who the best cook in the family was.

In all of our lives we look to believe in those that have come before us and in this family, she was certainly one of them, but she also looked back and believed in us.

I love you, and will miss you deeply along with the rest of this family and until our time comes, goodbye.

A. Kirk Williams, M. D.
12-25-2007

Discipline Is a Virtue

• •

(January 17, 2014)

Discipline is a trait of strength and honor, demanding multiple virtues from your very being, and one of the most admired and necessary traits of accomplishment needed in every dimension of your life—mental, emotional, spiritual and physical.

1.) The mental aspect of discipline remains one of the most challenging, for this is the control panel of your being. Likened to the effects of a virus infecting a computer, affecting your decisions from that point forward. The most complex and of course challenging is the unraveling process. How to undo, moderate, or simply discern truth from fiction as the socialization process is in full swing and perfected, if I may add. As mentioned before in previous articles, this is a complex process involving questioning of your own established platforms in life as they were assimilated from "whatever was on the table." Now that's all that we have an appetite for. Remember, how much of you is you, and how much is the regurgitation of you environment? Objective, forward, and firm thinking is a start. Tricky as it is, some conclusions reached will be painful, others rewarding, though still difficult to admit even to yourself. Having to uncover lies, exaggerated or modified truths that really are tall tales, will leave one in disbelief. "All my life I thought of myself as this way or that way" or "All of my life I felt like this or that"—now I see it is not so, pulling the rug right from under our feet.

The first step to solving a problem is first admitting that there is one, and keep in mind that a thousand-mile journey begins with the first step. Once you have the confidence to start connecting the dots, the truth will snowball, as they are all around you and have been for centuries. Some things just don't make sense, and for good reason, they don't add up. Kind of like math questions in school, in which the correct answers were provided in the back of the book. So with difficult questions, sometimes you would have to work backward to master the equations. . God or nature is that correct answer at the back of the book. Now work backward to understand where the lines are crossed, but please have the courage to address it once revealed. Oftentimes it will literally be the opposite of what you have built your life's foundation around, and therefore resisting and rationalization is expected, though, yes, it still can be a lie. Nevertheless, remember, your thinking and resolve remain all but a by-product of socialization, i.e., the wishes of men, not God.

2.) Spiritual discipline is of the heart, often overlooked and not shown nearly enough love as it provides the windows to our souls and has remained consistent since the dawn. Designed, programmed, and initiated by God, the laws of nature, unadulterated, unmanipulated, and unchanged, consistent principles likened to that rock when thrown up, it comes down, today, yesterday, yesteryear, and so on since the beginning. Forever present in every encounter as an underlying, soft, quiet, though, steadfast quality. Often filtering nonsense gathered by the mind and competing for favor, as this muscle, short of exercise, needs strengthening in us all, for way too often, it yields to all. Nevertheless, it does, however, provide us with that answer at the back of the book, in which we are to work back from in search of those crossed lines to, in effect, correct our thinking and subsequently our lives, for these are our Maker's true wishes.

3.) Emotional discipline usually follows the mind for it provides reaction to what the mind delineates as so. This is but another reason cited as to why mental discipline and correction is so important. Reacting inappropriately to even things divine as a result of errored input from the mind, despite highlighted correct answers. There are those occasions, however, when you feel something different than you think. This is the time for pause to unravel. Spiritual and mental elements are at odds as this represents conflict. Your God-given gifts are saying one thing, man's programming another. Intelligence speaks to a rational decision provided that all the circumstances, concerns, and alternative positions are fully evaluated.

4.) Physical discipline is everything from diet and exercise to overcoming addictions and restraining or modifying behavior as a result of inappropriate mental or emotional input as there are consequences for such. Commonly reflecting the net yield of the above equation involving mental, emotional, and spiritual discipline, as its product is produced. Nevertheless, easily recognizable is the physique that has followed the path of discipline, for it is symmetrical, lean, and muscular. There are striations in this group. However, naturally this is a difficult task requiring much planning, sacrifice, and downright making yourself follow a plan. And at its extreme example, tremendous discipline, sacrifice, and expense are also involved, literally a life-altering undertaking. Though many of us will just go through the motions, I suppose, to make ourselves feel better. Going to the gym daily, exercising year in and year out, yet seeing no results, most fully aware of why not, yet continuing to hide from the burden of modifying their diets.

For often, as mentioned above, overcoming addictions is a part requiring physical discipline as food represents a physical and psychological addiction. "I'm gonna work out today so I can have XYZ for dinner tonight." Nope, it doesn't work that way as evidenced by your results. And please don't misunderstand me. I feel your pain fully. The switch of discipline is not one of leisure. We live in America, where convenience is king and waiting at every corner is the opportunity to satisfy those taste buds for sweet and sour or simply an opportunity to calm those nerves as there are too many moving parts in our lives.

This all but repeats the same theme over and over again. Get a grip and develop this muscle of discipline for more and more its incorporation into our being is a necessary ingredient for basic healthy survival. All the lines, if allowed, will usually cross on the Truth. Magnify and respond appropriately to this message for it is a blessing and an answer to many of our prayers. The easy part is showing up and going through the motions; the difficulty begins when leaving. So from now on, when leaving the gym, the tough part is just beginning, watching your diet. So think to yourself, "Now, it's ab (abdominalis) time." Remember, discipline is a virtue.

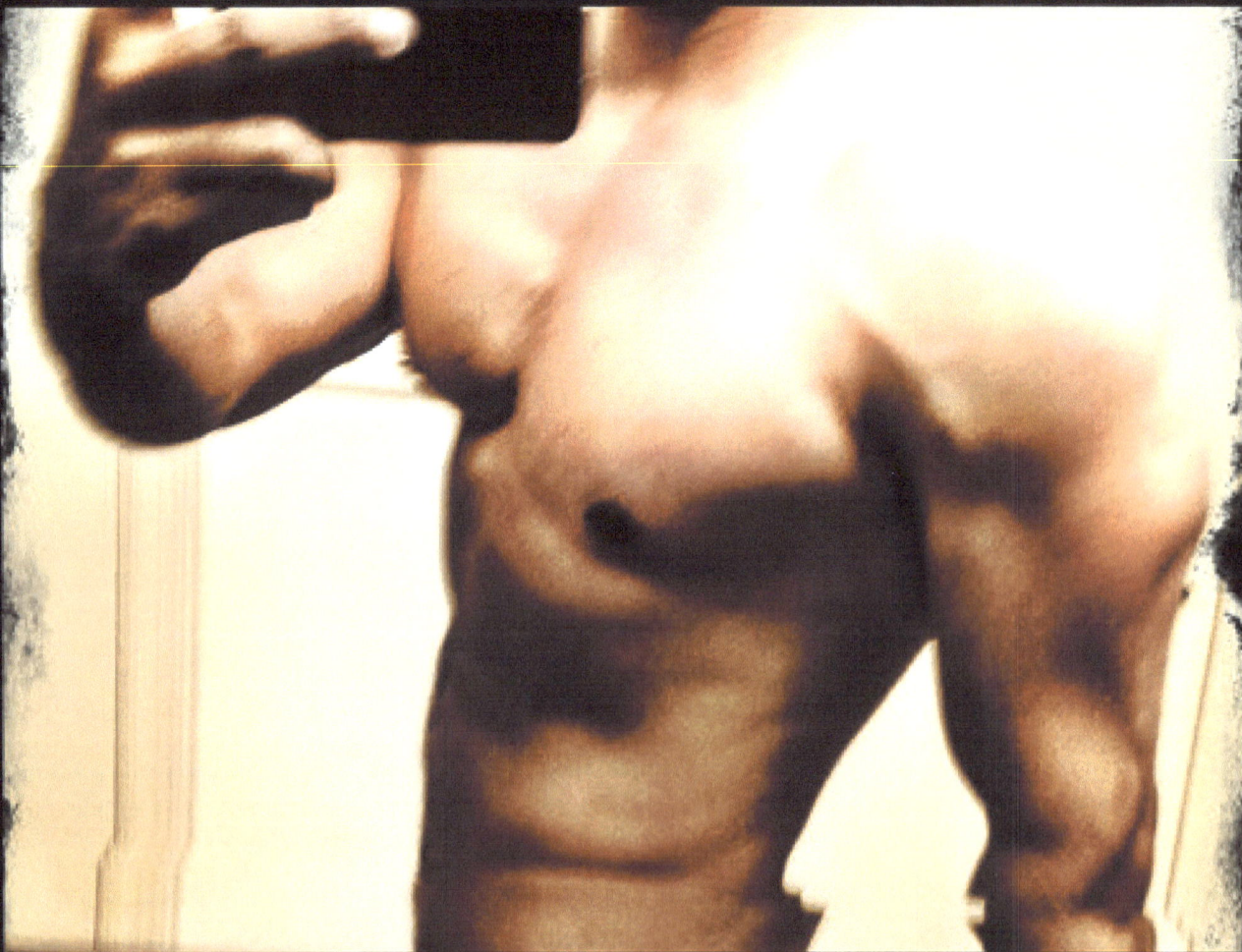

LIVING INSIDE OUR OWN BIOLOGY

(July 2013)

We are shaped and molded by an equation involving our life experiences overlying a pair of twenty-three chromosomes. Living inside a set of circumstances that ultimately creates the zone of comfort where we live most of our lives and thereby, as a by-product, ultimately sets the limits to our biology. Unbeknownst to ourselves, we mistakenly will evaluate others of different experiences, personal and otherwise, without recognizing the obvious, oftentimes different, realities. For now a different set of circumstances and challenges apply, leaving one with very little insight into these circumstances, as you have not been there and refuse to go. Drawing from a different well of experiences, never fully appreciating it as separate and different, which in turn limits your understanding or appreciation for others or their greatness. For they may have endured or achieved something we didn't, didn't think possible or simply didn't have the courage to pursue. How often do we say, "Hindsight is 20/20"? Kind of like "Now that I've had that experience, I have an appreciation for it now." This is but the same. Until you have had like experiences yourself, it can be very difficult to understand and even more difficult to truly understand that you really don't know. Offering your best seems like it "ought to be" or "should be" like this. When asked why, our reply is "Because"—*because* doesn't apply. What is missing , is enough common ground for overlap. Overlap enough to convey such meaning, and to this end renders a miscalculation at best, hence, the genesis of dispute.

Assuming all involved are rational and sound, no one wrong, just short of experience and therefore short of understanding. Open-mindedness demands something of us that in itself requires self-confidence, unselfishness, and courage in order to see past our own set of limits, beyond our own biology. Without proper background, simple math is a challenge; with it, calculus is a breeze. A child, adolescent, and adult can witness the same event yet see different things, all fully vested and certain of their experience, though all limited by their own biology.

It's within You

· ·

(Summer 2013)

When I was young and standing on the verge of understanding, I would often ask myself why. Why am I me? Why am I here? And why are all these people looking at me? As I appeared not fully vested in my understanding of the buried treasures, time revealed the source of truth. It resonates as the ideal gas law—perfect, consistent, and at peace with God, whatever you perceive him to be. America and our own personal prejudices keeps us from the truth. Thinking the answer is always some place that it's not, never realizing it's within you. Never empowering that one we overlook daily, thinking that it is always someone else or someplace else. Birth was given to us all by parents through the hands of God. Our genetics are from the dawn. Do not be confused. The blessings are within you.

BIAS IS FREE AND IN DISGUISE

· ·

(Summer 2013)

Bias is disguised, and unknowing to us all, a part of us all. Bias is based soundly in our biology overlayed by life experiences and conditioning, together creating our foundation in life,as we live every experience lived through twenty-three pairs of chromosomes. Those of us even blessed with intersections of our DNA, i.e. mother, father, sister and brother, even differ. Without even sufficient thought given to this context, we automatically assume "I've got this. I've got this because my position in society is superior to yours, based on some adopted often-changing equation of nonsense or just unknowing the true direction of the compass as it points north, unlike our assumption that it points east." Sit tight. None of us has ever considered there may be an outside to our inner self. Our thoughts and feelings represent all that we know and therefore nothing else can exist—this is not so. Each of the twenty-three has multiple options as they fall as they may, some dominant, some recessive, though all a blessing from God. Each selection represents a predisposition for an opinion, talent, or thought. A different expression of one or another of the same gene would yield a yes to a previous answer of no and likewise. Let's evaluate, not dismiss. As we sit and debate differences of opinion, we are doing nothing more than debating the differences of our flesh, biology, and DNA. Some perspectives are broader, more encompassing, , or should I just say "liberal" as their biology was programmed by an adjacent gene—nothing personal, it is just that way. As you gain perspective of the dynamics of this process, resolve is but a step away.

TALKING HEADS

• •

(December 18, 2013)

While tuned in to CNN/Piers Morgan the other day, performing some menial task around the house, my attention was drawn to the screen by the voice of Piers Morgan's guest, Ann Coulter, a right wing, conservative Fox News white female correspondent discussing the ethnicity of Santa Claus. This was a hotly debated topic the middle of December 2013, arising from comments made by Megyn Kelly, also a white female and a Fox News anchor. The week prior to Megyn Kelly and her guest, were discussing an article by Aisha Harris in which Harris described how Santa's consistent depiction as a white man made her feel uncomfortable and excluded as a young black girl in America. As her panelist began to broach the topic, Kelly made what she clearly thought was an important point: "And by the way, for all you kids watching at home, Santa just is white. But this person is maybe just arguing that we should also have a black Santa. But, you know, Santa is what he is and just so you know, we're just debating this because someone wrote about it, kids. Just because it makes you feel uncomfortable doesn't mean it has to change. You know, I mean, Jesus was a white man too. He was a historical figure; that's a verifiable fact—as is Santa, I want you kids watching to know that." These comments drew a tremendous backlash. After much criticism of her comments, Megyn Kelly responded with the "I was just joking" defense. As far as Jesus goes, Kelly did admit that it had been wrong for her to proclaim Jesus's whiteness. Jesus's race is "far from settled," she acknowledged. But she couldn't bring herself to say he wasn't white.

Somewhat in her defense, however, the United States does "claim" white people to be of European, Northern African, and Middle Eastern descent. This, I'm sure, is in an effort to also stake claims to the ownership of ancient Egypt and all its splendor, the biblical Garden of Eden with those two famous characters, Adam and Eve, as well as our current discussion, Jesus and his ethnicity. The former two subjects will be debated at a separate time. For now, our focus remains on Jesus. Keep in mind, however, that had no one raised concerns over her inaccurate comment regarding Jesus's whiteness, her comments would have been taken literally and accepted as truth, especially by those that don't know.

Likewise, Ann Coulter, a fellow Fox News commentator, or should I say, frequent guest exposing conservative dogma, also readily stated with defiance that Santa was white while acknowledging Kelly's comment of the same. Santa probably is white, but they both failed also to mention that he is a fictitious character. Piers Morgan's position, on the other hand, was that Santa could very well be multicultural depending on the lens. An Asian Santa for Asians, a Hispanic Santa for Hispanics, a black Santa for blacks, and so on, but she was adamant this was not the case and that he was white, period. Immediately following this discussion, the focus turned to the comment about Jesus's whiteness. I was anxious to hear this, but as expected from the previous discussion, it was predictable. Her position immediately was that it was obvious what color Jesus was, referring to the blond-haired, blue-eyed image we have all come to know that graces the walls of most sanctuaries throughout the world. Piers pressed her further into admitting this image was probably not accurate; however, conceding, her counter was that "Jesus was a Jew and probably beige in appearance" but "certainly not black." Never mind that Judaism is a religion and not a race of people of a specific color. Jesus was a Hebrew, and Hebrews of that day, the first century, populated Egypt, which is Greek for "land of the blacks."

I thought this was somewhat intellectually disingenuous in that those with the power of the pen and press should be more responsible in their opinions because of the impact that it has on the thought processes of people from all walks of life, but after thinking about it further, it dawned on me, that was exactly the intent. I was witnessing one of many of the historical tools that have been used for centuries to further advance the notion of white supremacy. A very powerful and effective tool, may I add, that has nearly perfected the art of mind control. Her comments were made with defiance and authority, and as a matter of fact, I admit that had I not been grounded in education and truth, this account sure would have sounded plausible to me. How many are not that are overwhelmingly influenced by such? And get this, as further discussion revealed, they both *knew* they were not representing the truth. Left unopposed, they would certainly have added another notch to the belt of white supremacy. Use yourself as an example as you read this article. Make note of your emotions, doubts, concerns, and affirmative or negative thoughts. Keep in mind these same tools are responsible for the shaping and molding of your attitudes regarding this subject, as well as the attitudes generated regarding self and the world as a whole—the machine of socialization. Try telling someone, anyone, regardless of race, that Jesus was of African descent and watch their response and even be prepared to duck to avoid their swing. This is but one example that illustrates the effectiveness of this powerful tool.

I am in no way claiming any level of expertise on such subjects, but I do just have two things to say—science and common sense. Mitochondrial DNA mapping and Y-chromosomal DNA mapping are more than not commonly used research tools of the modern era. Although far from the panacea, they do, however, provide significant information regarding the evolution of man that, coupled with carbon 14 radioisotope dating, all but eliminate much of the social debate and opinions generated by those that don't know. For example, a tidbit of information that is not widely distributed and certainly not widely discussed is the ethnicity of the original man, the African. Several years back, scientists published an article in *Scientific American* magazine that stated, among other things, that a large percentage—though I cannot recall the exact figure; I think in the 50–60 percent range—of current-day Earth's female population, utilizing mitochondrial DNA mapping technology, can be traced back to a single African female, irrespective of race. Likewise, the same article also published that utilizing Y-chromosomal DNA mapping technology, irrespective of race, a much smaller percentage of current-day males can also be traced to a single African male. Sure sounds like the biblical Adam and Eve.

I can distinctly recall a third-grade geography lesson in Mrs. Sutton's class, at M. W. Dogan Elementary school during the Christmas season, when I asked the question "Where was Bethlehem?"

As Mrs. Sutton pointed out Bethlehem's location on the globe, my first thought using third-grade logic, and I don't know why, was to make a mental note of Bethlehem's location and its relationship to the equator. Not knowing what I was feeling and certainly without confidence in what I was feeling, I was torn and confused. Raised not *on* but *in* the Bible belt, in Marshall, Texas, Jesus had blond hair and blue eyes, 'cause I saw him every Sunday at church. But this is how the truth, God's presence, works. I also knew that the closer you get to the equator, the hotter it gets as a result of increased exposure to UV radiation. The body's natural defense mechanism is to kink the hair and darken the skin. How then can someone whose people are indigenous to this area have blond hair and blue eyes? It's simple—they can't. It's not my call or your call but nature's or God's call. I've only told this story a handful of times, but every time I do, it continues to puzzle as well as amaze me that an eight—to nine-year-old had that kind of insight. Remaining is only one explanation—God, whatever you perceive him to be, has his hand on us all. Despite extensive socialization in one of the last counties in America to abolish slavery, Harrison county Texas, the truth, the natural laws of nature, i.e., the word of the God, resonated in the heart of a child. It took years for me to have the confidence to embrace this experience because no one I knew considered it even a remote possibility. In many of my literary works, I speak of dichotomies such as this as I have lived through many of them, and so have you. This is only the first I vividly recall. This is a real-life account by a child of the scripture that speaks to the fork in the road and spiritually and mentally following the one least traveled, following the truth. This experience is not unique to me. God has his hand on us daily, nudging us in his direction, but because our hearts are spiritually shallow, or should I say, lacking true confidence in his word as a result of such socialization, we follow what we are told and not what is real.

I know I've been there more than I care to admit, and unfortunately, living in America the concepts and beliefs we are forced to embrace and accept often draw consistent conflict with God's wisdom that I refer to as truth. The above examples are but two attempts of misguidance; in truth, those in the privileged positions of the power of the pen and press have fed untruths and notions of their superiority daily for centuries. Now a scientist and an adult, common sense speaks loudly to the natural laws of the planet as well as the flesh. God speaks to us daily, but we can't hear him because the world is so noisy with nonsense. The manmade trinkets, gadgets, and values fill our senses with desires to our detriment, not leaving room for substance and graciousness when presented. We have become so warped that the original vessel of our hearts and minds has become dismembered to the point they won't even accommodate true blessings when presented.

The injustice and inequalities suffered by people of color are and have always been palpable but especially those of African descent, the original man. How ironic. And that was what Ms. Coulter was saying in her unashamed and defiant response that "He surely wasn't black." But it's obviously okay to be anything else, so she chose "beige," yet she failed to realize even beige suggests African descent. Anyone with even a high school course in biology knows that genetic phenotypes range from recessive to dominant. Two whites can't produce a beige or black, only another white, but blacks can produce all the above. Why do some races have to feel superior to others? Is this not but a blatant example of racial insecurity, if I may? You know people in your everyday lives you define as haters or those that want what you have. This is no different. If it were not so, then there would be no hate. Despite elaborate explanations that have been propagated over time, it boils down simply to racial insecurity stemming from feelings of racial inferiority. This is not my doing or my belief but my interpretation of what has happened over time—should I say, my observance as the dots are connected.

Disingenuous as she has been, America has apologized to or made monetary reparations to every other race of people she perceives has been wronged, except those of African descent, not even a nod. I recall an incident of my best friend, an accomplished orthodontist that, by most of our standards, doesn't look like a doctor because he celebrates his God-given attributes by embracing his kinky hair that he wears in what we refer to as a "nappy 'fro." One day while rushing in and out of the Galleria shopping mall in Houston, running behind as he so often does to pick up a couple of items, he accidentally bumped into a young Asian fella and his daughter. No one was even remotely close to being harmed. Being the gentleman and professional he is and has always been all his life, he apologized profusely. This Asian fella, obviously new to this country, speaking fragmented English barely audible, commenced into a verbal tirade that ended with "Go back to hood." To finish the story, security was called, and all the witnesses, black and white alike, supported my friend with an accurate account of what occurred. But what right did this immigrant have to treat an American citizen with such indignity and feel it totally appropriate? He doesn't even realize that the freedoms he has in this country right now come from the struggles of people that look like my friend that he has so little respect for. No need to ask why because the negativities regarding people of color are pervasive throughout our society. Reading between the lines, the two above discussions are but examples, again. If such indignities occurred to others on a daily basis, things would change quick, fast and in a hurry. However, it occurs mainly because they have created and maintained this stage over time.

It is so ever apparent in our society that those with the power of the pen and press think they can just say how they think things are to be and magically they are. Yet on Sunday mornings they are praying to God but all the time playing God. Here in the state of Texas recently, the Board of Education decided they didn't like the way the story of slavery was being taught and told, so they decided several years back to change it. They changed the story because it makes them "look bad," and they did. Never mind that it's the truth. Does this sound familiar? In the above discussion Megyn Kelly made the important point that changing history or historical figures should not be just because it makes you uncomfortable. But now it's okay for the Texas Board of Education to *change the history of slavery* because it makes them, whites, "look bad." Which one is it, or should it be modified to say it can be either or depending on when it's to their advantage? History is not theirs to change. History is what it is, but what we are witnessing again is a reflection of the founding fathers in these people attempting to set or create the world according to them, irrespective of the truth, or should I say, inconsistent with the wisdom of our Maker. Kind of like winding a rubber band as tight as you can and daring it to unwind once released. They think that by changing the story, the impact, circumstances, and conditions created by over four hundred years of indentured servitude and savagery are erased, never even considering a diplomatic, respectful approach to such indignity.

This indignity, as with injustice all around the globe, is like that wound rubber band. You can dare it all you want not to unwind once it's released, but to no avail. So too is human nature.

Now, get this and fast forward, anyone that raises any questions regarding these well-documented indignities is considered a radical or rebel, something derogatory, but the system and people that perpetrated these horrific crimes against mankind are considered decent human beings despite such

savagery. Go figure. So the discussion the other night with Ann Coulter and the other day with Megyn Kelly, although some ten or fifteen minutes, extended deep into the bowels of time, suffering, injustice, and inequalities of human history. Let's just tell it the way we want it to be and use our position of authority to propagate our will, and no one will know. Those with a broader spiritual base could never fathom such, though many are far from such spiritual corruptness. Everyone rests assured the differences are known and clear. Just something to think about.

THE LAWSUIT

. . . .

(January 04, 2014)

Few experiences in life demands giving of resources intensely on all levels for extended periods of time—mental, emotional, spiritual, professional, personal, financial, and physical sacrifice—exhausting literally, and not just a punch line to impress the reader. Most never even remotely experiencing a like experience, maybe likened to preparation for the biggest test of your life that you would spend one to two months intensely preparing for and all that you are and have worked for hanging in the balance—failure unthinkable. Now let's maintain that daily intensity for over three and a half years while attempting to maintain balance, sanity, and health as the corporation manipulates the environment to purposefully interfere with your ability to feed your family.

Several years back, in isolation, I faced exactly that. Feeling wronged and was in a big way for doing the right thing as evidenced by the outcome, though daily we all face this bully, those bigger than ourselves—the corporations, public opinion, the bosses with the power of the pen that schedule our work and ultimately manipulate and control our livelihood. However, I must say, regardless of circumstances, usually the resources of the company versus the little guy will win hands down, and they usually are filthy, dirty, and wrong—how unfortunate and just *WRONG* . My ordeal was a little different in that I had a few more resources than most, as well as personal experience in the corporate board room. Yet still, while standing in a deafening silence, alone, my knees buckled more than once, so I fully appreciate the odds of the average everyday person seeking and receiving any level of satisfaction legally when wronged by their employer, the corporations of the world. Furthermore, I also hate to disappoint you, but the US government whom you think "is by the people and for the people" is not. I know it's a bitter pill to swallow, but it's the truth. So essentially, you are on your own, just you and Jesus. As the corporate bosses fly around on the corporate jets, confident, smoking cigars, jet-setting and literally laughing, fully enjoying your misfortune, especially when you look like me, can be demoralizing if you allow it to be. This served to fortify my determination and recommitment over and over again. Utilizing the resources of the company as their own, the lawyers, the perks, never missing a pay period, family dinner, or vacation—all is well as they plot and plan among themselves with every intention of destroying your life and everyone in it. My world couldn't have been further in the opposite direction. Fear, anxiety, insecurity, and isolation are my new best friends. Certainly, if you are at odds with the bosses, the corporation, you must have done something wrong—you had to. Despite having never heard a single explanation or an ounce of insight into the situation, now immediately conclusions are drawn, and they are the gospel because Mickey Mouse has raised his head and the enslaved minds that service the corporate massa are engaged.

We are told throughout life to stand up for what we believe in and do the right thing—except the circumstances in dispute happens to be a friend of the one that controls the power of the pen that schedules your work, or the guy at the bank that decides whether your mortgage is approved, or the teachers and principal that educate your kids, or the grocery store supervisor that may or may not extend credit until the next pay period, or the police officer who just all of a sudden now has a suspicion as he exercises his right to stop you repeatedly at the same intersection daily, and so on and so forth. Are you sure you have a circumstance to dispute, or were you just joking? The worldly ramifications are spelled out, concede and surrender. Reacting to the conflict in my heart, God left me with no choice, even though man had threatened on every front, as they said, "I thought you were just joking." But your decency and divineness knows right from wrong, for if you were not supposed to feel mistreated, disrespected, and wronged, you wouldn't, so you are. Kind of like the winding of a rubber band and daring it to unwind when released, dare all you want; you know what's going to happen once released—human nature is but the same. For every action there is an equal and opposite reaction, especially when you are spiritually rooted.

Again you face the fork in the road and again you choose to follow the road less traveled, for this path is the Maker's preference and now *you* are chosen to follow. Being spiritually rooted, the choice is not yours to make; it is, however, made for you.

Now I was at the front and center of the biggest legal battle of my life with absolutely no support. My lawyer that also doubles as one of my dearest friends, a handful of close friends and family members, that was it, as a whole professional community, main street and the works, were in opposition. I'm fighting a battle for the little guy, but I'm the bad guy; even under my own roof, support was scarce. Despite all the negatives, God filled my heart with strength, courage, determination, and wisdom. My father often said, "It's easy to go to a party and have fun, but it's when the chips are down that true character is shown." As the soil is lifted from the ground to dig the foxholes of life, choices are made regarding who enters with you. We make these choices at times of peace and love while embracing idealism, never proven, all theoretical, kind of like the party. Now when needed, the rubber is giving way to the road.

The fun began as the corporation played all the games and performed all the tricks a well-funded company could muster, to expend as many coins as possible from the kitchen table, corporate dollars versus my dollars, as a matter of "strategy." Threats, lies, and rumors assisted and curried by those that used to pat you on the back as a gesture of close friendship and were now leading the charge for your demise. Others straddled the fence, hoping to benefit personally somehow from your misfortune, and those under your own roof, cold and unfriendly. Because apparently I was already written off as defeated; most couldn't wait to bare their teeth, revealing their true feelings, but get this, I already knew, for throughout my life, that sixth sense has forever blessed me. After much to-do, postponements, and unnecessary costly to-dos, we finally saw our day in court. The corporation marches in with stacks and stacks of boxes filling nearly every seat in the courtroom, a team of lawyers and corporate vests, video cameras with the backdrop on their side, and a very big to-do. On the flip side was only my lawyer and me seated at a small desk with our binders, stickys, pen and pencils, and a pullback for my dreads. But get this, again this is how the truth works.

Four weeks later, the truth favored us 12–0 in one case and 11–1 in another. Yes, my attorney is very good at what he does, and I am a different kind of client, but we both had faith and verbalized going in that truth, and above all, God was on our side. You see, we all want to be like Jesus when nothing is required of us other than conversation or pontification. How quickly it changes when it's truly time to roll up our sleeves, against all odds, with no apparent victory in sight, and be like Jesus. Confronting the faces of wickedness and evil as you are armed only with truth and fully willing to pay with blood, sweat, and tears, if not your life. It's as interesting as it is ironical, how the so-called churchgoers can stand right beside you and see or feel nothing as they go through the motions daily and twice on Sundays, praying to Jesus.

This verdict was front-page headline news of several newspapers in our area, though it was bittersweet. You see, this represented nearly three years of my life, preoccupied daily, anxious, uncertain, doubted, doubting, abandoned, depleted, forgotten, yet believing. These are three years of preoccupation gone forever. What role does such adversity ultimately play in your mental, emotional, spiritual, and physical health? It matters not when you are called, as above. It's not your call to make; it's made for you. For church is in you. It's not just to be talked about but to be lived, and lived it was. On the contrary, it's not just about the money. It is, however, about the truth and the journey that provides a lens to refine your forward vision and thinking and to provide a platform to reevaluate your positions in life, reminding you that among other things, hell is for purification and no values are possible without strength. This experience had precipitated more than I wanted to confirm even though I already knew, but confirmation is final. As the victory bell rang, all came running—"I knew you had it," "Congratulations," "I was with you all the way"—as I nodded in disbelief. Some people have no conscience and make no bones about it. Just made that way, I suppose, truly reflective of a narrow spiritual base. An even bigger problem for me personally, now, is how to restore the hollowness of my soul as I have given so much that few can appreciate. David versus Goliath, the little guy versus the billion-dollar corporation. This was not supposed to happen, because it so rarely does. Remembering all the experts that so often talk tough and smart and hold themselves out as an authority, would they have the courage to see through an ordeal such as this? Though they think of themselves as "soldiers" high and mighty as long as only talking, posturing, and pontificating are involved—you be the judge. It takes courage to stare life in its face and see it for what it really is. But so states the scripture, and it's true, "Know the Truth for the Truth will set you free." Another way of saying it, according to George Clinton and Funkadelics back in the day, "Free your mind and your Ass will Follow." Few, and I mean few, have no to very little appreciation for my struggle and perseverance. In fact, in some respects, it's almost like sleeping with the enemy. I've come to embrace the life of a soldier and all that it entails, up to and including being misunderstood by those of the many different orders. Unbeknownst to them, I and others like me fought for many of their freedoms as they stand with chest out, exposing to be an expert yet scared to death of the real world. As one of my dear friends used to say, "If they had to walk a day in our shoes, their hearts would just stop beating." He's right.

been focused and committed daily since leaving high school, doing everything right, but apparently too proud and just a little too full of optimism. Many of our brothers and sisters have succeeded in spite of themselves, overcoming greater odds ever given credit for and so many times, really, given no help. They are the bad guy every step of the way, until they crescendo, then everyone finds and embraces them, none to be found as they struggled and fought in the trenches alone. My father used to always say, it's not just about the level you reach in life but it is, however, about the obstacles you have overcome to reach those goals. Two men standing side by side, mirroring accomplishments, can be greatly separated by the circumstances leading to this feat, one far more successful on every level than the other we all need to recognize.

Music Is a Single Succession of Tones, Single or Combined

(Winter 2013)

Music is a special instrument of nature that reaches far within our souls, never ambivalent, always available, and with memory that is exact.

Music is a special instrument of nature that reaches the hearts of all with melodies that are as broad as all.

Music is a special influence of nature that reaches the old and new as the rhythms of life give way from pitter-patter to a slow waltz that now ails.

Music is a special instrument of nature that provides refuge to the wounded and life to the near life's end.

How clever are sounds that accurately present images that smile, speak, and touch our being in every way as only it can.

The balanced rhythm and harmony waltzes with a syncopated beat mixed with staccato at its best, only to emerge as your life inside a song.

Music is a special instrument of nature that never leaves you outside of yourself.

I now know why birds fly south for winter and salmon spawn in the chilled waters upstream—it's the beat within the rhythm of is.

The midcycle ovum, with all its circumstance, awaits its fate, as it has since the dawn. Miracle, no; orchestrated, yes.

Feel the bass as it defines and gives texture to the lows, as does the soprano and strings color the highs, space between that fills to further embody your life inside a song. All apart yet together plays as one.

Our grade-school music teacher once taught us all: "Music is a single succession of tones, single or combined."

FRIDAY NIGHT CHILLIN'

(August 2013)

Friday night chillin', alone in a room full of mirrors, time traveling, reflecting. Echoes from the past fill the room in 3-D as the jukebox mixes your favorite tunes—what a treat. Special events, faces, aromas, places, and spaces out there are recreated by that or those special tunes that freeze the frame, allowing one to relive times now past, though very alive. Heartstrings plucked as an ensemble of melodies appear that have survived the test of time. A magic carpet that steals you away to simple times of profound meaning and less complexity, times that reflect a foundation grown now into you.

Music, a Special Instrument of Nature

(July 2013)

Music is a special instrument of nature that kisses your heart, stimulates your mind, and strengthens your soul. Tunes that reach far within you to retrieve that little one, the young one you used to be. Pure at heart in search of adolescence or young adulthood as the birds chirp and the bees swarm into a cloud of joy. Sharing new love, anticipating what's to come. Overjoyed, as morning is but a nap away, and another day awaits that special smile, walk, and perhaps some play.

KIRK WILLIAMS

PERCH ON SUNDAYS

EVERYBODY LOVES THE SUNSHINE

(August 2013)

A fall day in Northeast Texas, probably late September, the leaves with only a flash of autumn, as school has just begun. Now a high school junior, I had just moved back home to small-town America after being away in Houston for three years while my father completed law school. I was reunited with all those relationships that extended from my childhood. It was truly exciting. Wiley College was located in my hometown and served as a central focus in our community for every generation and at this point in time, however, our generation was interested only in weekend parties every weekend. This particular year, the fall of '76, the neighborhood fellas reunited, ages extended from high school to college and beyond. We formed a group called OTHG, short for Over-the-Hill Gang, because we grew up and lived in a close proximity to one another over the hill. Wiley also had a radio station, KBWC, that kept us up to date on the latest tunes.

This particular weekday evening, an hour or two before sundown, I happened through campus, listening to the radio while driving and leaning in my newly acquired green Toyota Celica, proud as can be. Hair braided in neat rows to the back, length of course, allowing accumulation along my lower neck. Dressed in blue jeans, blue T-shirt with white writing that uttered nothing, and brown earth shoes to cap it off. Can't forget the "cool" matching faded-lens sunglasses, fading darker from top to bottom, and I had all the colors from rose to gray and special blue this day. Seventy-degree early-fall crisp weather, college students scattered on the yard, some standing along the drive, others seated on a raised embankment atop an incline overlooking parked cars on the side of the road, all with windows down, tuned in to KBWC.

While cruising the incline, vision-scanning the area from behind tinted lenses all but accented an image etched in the annals forever, natural high if I may. Suddenly, a song like I had never heard before descended from the heavens: "My life, my life, my life, my life . . . in the sunshine", fashioned over xylophones and harmonized female background vocals. It hit a cord that resonates today, nearly paralyzing me. Immediately I was captured by this beautiful scenic moment as my attention was drawn to the canopy of trees behind the seated students, admiring the orange sunrays and blunt shadows as they hit the ground, creating the backdrop for a picture-perfect end to a beautiful autumn day. Music echoed from all directions as our space filled with beams glowing like extensions of the sun. This was my very first exposure to such an arrangement, and it sent me into orbit as if we were all in a dream that slowed and lasted for a lifetime. This experience only served as a reminder that still, even today, everybody loves the sunshine.

WEEKEND TREATS BACK IN THE DAY

(July 2013)

Donald and Daffy Duck had very little on Roadrunner and Wylie Coyote. Next comes Scooby Doo with a Scooby snack. Saturday mornings were a treat, every week, to a youngster not so steep. Weekends kicked off with the Bradys followed by *The Partridge Family, Odd Couple*, and *Love American Style*, so protect your favorite seat. Friday night tradition was nothing if without oven-fresh chocolate-chip cookies and a glass or two from Elsie's hind tit. Morning is but a nap away, awaiting is a Scooby snack because "Roadrunner, beep-beep, the Coyote's after you." Spaaaaaace ghooooost, Superman, and the other super friends are making way for Yosemite Sam spazzing out over that smart-ass of a Wabbit. Tom tricking out Jerry as Mike and the J5 make it so we "Never can say Goodbye." Early '70s were the bomb. Cartoons dead-ended into little league football or basketball, depending on the season, followed by marbles and a motorbike ride. Saturday evening parties awaiting young fellas competing for the biggest 'fro and highest heels covered perfectly by a bell-bottomed flow. Stevie, Marvin, Barry, J5, and War providing all-day music. Rich are these times with nutrients that served in the creations of you. Intersecting are the crossroads of time where first experiences remain unchanged as if frozen in time for, as Gladys would say, the very benefit of the "makings of you."

Sweet, Sticky Thing

· ·

(August 2013)

Sweet, sticky thing . . . A tune that caught me square in the middle of adolescence, fifteen. A memory that lives in my heart today. Recalling a time in the fall of '75 just after completion of driver's education, not quite sixteen but could drive with someone licensed in the front seat. A beautiful crisp October day now turning to evening. The sun was a heavy orange glow resting peacefully on the horizon, its surroundings colored blue. Shadows blunt as in the fall with leaves changing and still as they paint the landscape oh so real. I convinced my mom to allow me to drive her to the movies at Gulfgate Mall so my cousin and I could ride through town with the windows down and lean like a pair of clowns. A special emotion, thought of time and hope. Rejoicing in the crispness as the theater is near and our autumn ride was oh-so dear.

Deeper and Deeper

· ·

(July 2013)

Deeper and deeper I go into the audiophile, into the tunes surrounding the most indelible of times. Hearing and seeing for the very first time visions that glowed, illuminating feelings never known until that time, never before or since equaled. Accumulated as a body of fabric sewn into a miracle of blessings, we continually use for cover and comfort as we visit and revisit from time to time. Providing needed therapy and refuge, as strength is drawn for purpose, the purpose of hope.

SUNDAY MORNINGS

· ·

(Spring 2013)

The complexity of the message is met with ambivalence and a distinct notion of impropriety. However, in the face of continued shrinking spiritual confidence, the lie is still honored despite our commitment to the most segregated day of the week, Sunday mornings. As it is colored with a face, we have accepted through conditioning that it is just and fair, though it is not. The wiring of our minds and souls has accepted the incongruence, even though nature poses an alternative solution. Fear of persecution prevails by those with the power of the pen, so we choose not to follow the road less traveled but its alternative, clearly a variance from scripture. And then wonder why conditions of our lives are unacceptable as we pray daily for deliverance. Never mind the obvious choices of church we routinely choose to ignore because acknowledgment would demand stepping out of zones of convenience and comfort, all while rationalizing, in the same breath, I wanna be like Jesus, "WoW," go figure. Again, as we continue to pray seeking self-improvement, forgetting or never fully appreciating, "He only helps those that help themselves." If Sunday morning worship is to truly ring in our ears, so then should our courage to follow his path. .

It Flows

• •

(Spring 2013)

It flows 'cause it's real, though I am told it's a lie. Walk away 'cause it's easier, and join us as we perpetrate a fraud, so we think, against the very hand that molded us. Why give such a choice to those so unworthy? It puzzles the beast as he bleeds.

A Soldier's Life

• •

(Spring 2013)

A soldier's work is never done, for it is not his life to have, only to share. Torn between the contemporary and ancient world, his path is clear.

Manipulation

• •

(Spring 2013)

Not what you want the truth to be but what it truly is as set forth by the big bang. We are lied to and manipulated daily by the weakest of the weak for their gain, financial or otherwise. With every parting of her lips, America hides from her past.

Contemplation

• •

(Spring 2013)

At a place situated someplace between the beginning and the end and having witnessed all the frailties of choice, the beast contemplates his plight.

AMERICA

• •

(Spring 2013)

America parts her lips and tells us who she wants to be, not who she is, in an attempt to erase the memory of her roots. Visible and tangible its theories prevail even though with increased odds of failure as it challenges, not embraces, the order set forth by the one that preceded us all.

Upon Awakening

· ·

(Spring 2013)

Upon awakening every morning, one of our first thoughts should be "What can I do today to improve my condition?" Oftentimes we fail to recognize we have already been blessed with many of life's answers as they live with us daily. Our challenge is to embrace them and follow that path. Having replaced God's or nature's values with assimilated ones, out of our own doing, we fail to follow. Ignoring the spiritual compass, we have lost perspective and direction; our struggle is not with others, places, or things but with oneself. In the end and at its highest peak, this experience we define as life amounts only to one thing—personal growth. Be all you can be in every dimension of your life. Completeness is the objective as set forth by our Maker, always "He who conquers himself is the greatest warrior." Our ship may arrive three or four times in a lifetime only to be missed because we can't swim and refuse to learn or are afraid of the small life raft needed to carry us a short distance from shore. We are not willing to extend beyond our comfort zone yet fully expecting to grow. A law-abiding citizen shouts from the crowd, "Stop standing in your own way!" Even he knows God has his hand on us all.

Happy Birthday, Granddaddy

(July 4, 2013)

As I sit under the big oak, enjoying the morning breeze and remembering the smell and sounds of the crushed white shell as cars pass, leaving behind a tunnel of white dust, coupled with the contrasting smell of freshly cut grass, I marvel at the perfectly manicured grounds as though it is a work of art. While anxiously awaiting the arrival of extended family, I see a familiar sight in the morning shade underneath the formosa tree—the old man reclining on his favorite green and white nylon, wiping beads from his brow. He has completed his morning chores. Nevertheless, remaining is that mask of sour on his face as it gives way to piercing blue eyes. In the distance you can hear Grandmother complaining to her sons and daughters alike about Daddy's antisocial behavior, but rest assured that as the grandkids arrive, that look of sourness would give way to a large gesture of approval, and so it was. Grandmother was always right. Embracing times now past though very alive. Happy birthday, George Joseph Veazey Sr. (7/4/1894–6/13/1988).

After the Family Picnic

• •

(July 5, 2013)

Yesterday those that came before us touched our lives and hearts once again as they so often do. Although young and without the benefit of life's trials and tribulations, my heart has always favored those times. Feelings of love have transcended the years, an anchor deep in the fabric of my soul that's held steady and afforded me a foundation of self, a sense of belonging, and the confidence to reach in whatever direction that favors the sun, despite being often alone and against all odds. Now many of us are blessed with our own families and afforded the benefit of contrast as we recognize from our own efforts and struggles what it must have been like for those that came before us. None since have raised eleven children, and it's still just about impossible to get all at the table at once. Our reflection is about just that, not only their kids but the thirty-five grandkids and greats as well. This is no small feat. In fact, it remains a celebration of life in which we all played a role. Special as it was, our clocks are ticking—our little ones' chances or now little ones' little ones' chances to experience this extension of their flesh windows are slowly closing as we watch. Let's challenge one another now that we the young have become the old, to do this at least once again with the same zest and zeal for those that come behind us.

Curves

• •

(Summer 2013)

Life throws us all curves, which I welcome because it takes us to a different room with different art, smell, presentation, and texture. Without it *that* inside, to our inner self would never be experienced, restricting the zenith of life. We are all equipped with the resources to succeed. Do not just speak of faith but walk in it. Only then is his message completely realized.

The Trajectory

• •

(Summer 2013)

Greatness is a blessing kissed by the sun at the dawn, with years on the planet, however, the trajectory will slow and become palpable, predictable, and clear. Our faces rejoice as in the presence of fresh air as the veil is removed, revealing some secrets and answers to the chemistry of life. My friend once told me he was going to the sun. I said, "But, my brother, you're gonna burn up." His reply was "No, because I'm going at night." Art comes as it pleases, as it appeals to our hearts and senses as that little pearl lodged between that loose plank and the floor, forever present, as it reveals itself only to our surprise.

IN SEARCH OF

● ●

(2008)

Everything in nature seeks its Maker. Small ducklings upon birth will follow movement in search of their mother. So does man in pursuit of his Maker. We look for God in experiences, nature, and most of all, each other. The wisdom of the Creator in teaching and in being is a part of us all. Whether conscience or otherwise, the more godly a person, the greater our attraction, likened to flakes of metal in a magnetic field, never even aware of the greater force that constantly blesses our very being. "I don't know why I feel the way I do about that person, but I do." We are nothing more than pawns of creation to be shifted and altered as the Creator allows. Who are we to question the wisdom of his compositions? If you care to know more about an artist, you study his works. Notice the subjects, textures, colors, and strokes—all different to the untrained eye yet revealing to the refined one. Allow it to take and move you as it pleases. Explore the masterpiece for it is of the kingdom of God.

EINSTEIN—HE ALREADY KNEW

• •

(2008)

Let's employ that ancient philosophical thought process defined as logic. We have all at least seen the globe that represents the third planet from the sun known by most as Mother Earth, our home. Now recall an image of the big blue marble as seen from outer space and hold it. Best we can tell nothing is coming out, or nothing is going in. Therefore, all that is here has always been here, including us; "ashes to ashes, dust to dust" defines a simple perennial aspect of this cosmic experience that has remained consistent. Einstein explained much of it with his theory of relativity ($E = mc2$), i.e., matter is neither created nor destroyed; it just changes forms. Before this explanation, however, was it no less true? It is what it is. As with higher learning, usually the answers are always in the back of the book. Given the correct answer, it remains your challenge to master life's equation.

DIFFERENT BY DESIGN

(2008)

Dissect the anatomy of our culture and dissect the nature of the beast that we are. Simply realizing the key to understanding others is to first understand yourself. This accomplishment unlocks the key that opens the hearts of others for full disclosure. If someone steps on your foot, you know how it feels. You in turn know how it feels when someone else has their foot stepped upon. Empathy is a subjective tool that allows corporation among all that may have at least a glimpse into their rudimentary, ancient being. All the answers are there. You don't use a hammer to screw in a screw or a screwdriver to hammer in a nail. The proper instrument will suffice, and it is efficient. The Creator has already made us finely attuned with something in mind. We are at our best when we walk hand in hand with what he intended for us. For example, men and women were not created equally or intended to be; if so, they would have been. A woman will evaluate the world of a man from a physiological, psychological, and even physical perspective known only to her and vice versa. Dressed in their finest intellectual attire, both can gather around the round table and never fully convey to one another truly conditions of their flesh. No words will ever convey in totality or even partially the sensation of monthly pelvic cramps or the experience of preparation the female body undergoes as it prepares to bring forth new life. Men live completely outside these experiences, to name only a few. Likewise, men have those experiences unique only to them that no line of reasoning or discussion will ever convey. Simply, anticipate things that are reachable or sound. Oftentimes, literally from inception, defeat is a foregone conclusion because the anticipated objectives are not possible. Mentally, emotionally, and spiritually, there is an optimum zone. Our challenge is to find that zone and stay there, where all the essential nutrients needed for mental, emotional, and spiritual growth are available in abundance, mainly truth.

THEMES IN LITERATURE

(2008)

  As in literature and so with life, multiple themes exist; namely, man versus nature, man versus man, and the last of which remains the most challenging, man versus himself. Man versus nature has its place. Today, however, it is more like man is at combat with nature, and how is she fighting back? Her fury comes by way of hurricanes, earthquakes, tornadoes, cyclones, floods, tsunamis, wildfires, deadly diseases, etc. We really should have more respect for our mother than we do. What characteristics of the beast allow such behavior then rationalize it completely? To be on the knowing end of destroying God's creation with such zest and zeal is spiritually ill. This remains a losing proposition for all of mankind, not just biting the hand that feeds you but also destroying and melting it away with acidic and caustic substances. Mother Earth has blessed us all with life, and our eternal thanks reflects a totally irresponsible posture that robs her of resources, natural and otherwise, that are being used to her detriment as well as our own.

  Man versus man, however, encompasses the preponderance of the human experience. Battles are fought near and far that depict unimaginable violence. However, in this modern era of legal exploitation, commonly man versus man is lived throughout the courts of the land. No one is ever responsible. It constantly remains the doing of someone else. If this is the claim and you, the plaintiff, is never responsible and you, the defendant, also a product of this society, is also not responsible, then who is responsible? The judge, perhaps, who too is the product of this guiltless society, certainly remains flawless and neutral. Someone has to be responsible other than myself, "'cause I'm not." There are tales of obese people that have legally pursued McDonald's for their weight gains, yet McDonald's has never been on record as force-feeding anyone. Fault also has to be shared by the physicians that in due course will also fail at managing the multiple health conditions that will arise out of this population, never mind lack of patient compliance. No, the fault obviously lies at the feet of the individual defined as lack of self-control or lack of self-discipline, which clearly falls without objection into the category of man versus himself.

  Many of the ills of our society begin and end between our own ears. You live life through yourself. All that is experienced comes from within; all the treasures we desire are neatly packaged and organized into a being known as you. Think for a moment: Your vision is the brain's interpretation of absorbed light by the retina. The sensation of touch or feel is a tactile stimulus that is collected and packaged by skin or nerve receptors then transmitted as an impulse to the brain for interpretation. What you smell, taste, or even hear are too packaged and processed by the brain. The joy of sex, love, and happiness as

well as its opposites all too comes from within. The illusion is that it is all exogenous—not so. Your mind and body simply interprets and processes exogenous stimuli that ultimately will speak to you in a language that is understood by all. Very little reasoning of an open and objective mind dispels any notion of fiction. Most of the battles not fought enough are when it comes to us dealing with ourselves. It is a complete and total library of knowledge that yields more than the value of money, gold, or silver, for it is not for sale but obtainable during quiet times of self-analysis. Sure, battles are and will forever be fought among one another. However, the greatest battle of all starts and ends with you. "He who conquers himself is the greatest warrior."

COMMERCIALS: MY PRODUCT IS THE BEST—NO, MINE IS—NO, MINE IS . . . NONSENSE?

(January 14, 2014)

How is it even remotely possible that every product advertised is the best? Turn on the tube and the same kind of product of a different company is better than all the others. Each one better than the other. Somehow that's hard to believe, and for good reason, because it's not possible. Know what I mean? Again, pervasive nonsense sanctioned by the whole as just business or marketing. Never mind that it is also a known lie yet rationalized as acceptable or okay even while in the midst of prayer. Wow. Most principles of our society, having deep roots in capitalism, leave very little room for honor. Make what you can and as much as you can regardless of consequence. We have no regard for others, earth, or God yet bend our knees in prayer—for what? Without a conscience or little concern thereof, this is what we have come to, and we call this progress.

TRUTH

•••••••••••••••••••••••••••

(2008)

Truth knows only one way. It cares not how you feel about it, or anyone else, or anything else for that matter. It is all-knowing, consistent, and brutal, yet fair that represents the closest concept to what we know as magic. It is said, "Know the truth for the truth will set you free." What does this mean to you? Does this appeal to your better judgment, sound good, or simply provide the author an opportunity to impress the reader? Let's take a real-life situation and examine its application. A person presents to the emergency room experiencing shortness of breath. The emergency room physician examines the patient and decides he is experiencing shortness of breath as a result of heart failure and treats him as such when in fact the person is having difficulty breathing secondary to an exacerbation of COPD (emphysema). In this particular instance, the emergency room physician has a particular interest in heart patients and continues to misread the data to, in effect, create a heart case. The patient, however, continues to deteriorate, requiring further intervention and eventual intubation with respiratory support. Better diagnostic capability and objectivity could potentially have avoided the entire ordeal. However, oftentimes we too see only what we want to see or fail to interpret the apparent if it doesn't coincide with our desires. This happens daily and pervades every dimension of our life. This person nearly lost his life. What has it cost you? Marriage, family, friends, job, sanity, material wealth, or just spiritual well-being—as the list continues.

THE REVOLUTION

· ·

(2008)

We also have to recognize our prejudices. As I sit and write at this very moment, I am the product of twentieth—and twenty-first-century socialization. Like everyone of my era, there is a wish list of desired things to, in effect, bequeath upon me supreme happiness—my own home, wife and kids, television, car, furniture, and the list goes on and on. The industrial revolution in its entire splendor yielded as a by-product a society of selfish, insensitive constituents. This is not all the fault of the constituents. However, if this capitalistic experiment was performed anywhere on the planet, human behavior being as it is, consistent, with few exceptions, the results would probably be the same. We must look at ourselves and slowly realize our selfishness, weaknesses, and insecurities as individuals. At least acknowledge the concept to ourselves. The first step to solving a problem is first admitting there is one. Truly this may represent a move in the right direction—direction of self-awareness and understanding the person you are. Ultimately getting to know oneself on a mental, emotional, and spiritual level yields great dividends by way of self-confidence, self-awareness, and self-esteem. Concomitantly, it's that very experience or journey into self that awakens the early man that lives within you. Fruits of creation, as well as a to-do list, await you as you return time and time again for comfort and a smile.

It Is, However, in You

(2008)

It all times is very difficult to get individuals to acknowledge their own shortcomings, especially if the existing foundation that supports their ideologies and way of life is to their advantage, whatever they perceive that to be. Negotiations and overall goodwill would flourish if all the smart and powerful people would just sometimes lend an ear and their heart. It never ceases to amaze me when someone is giving an account of their life or of a revelation in which they have had something different and unique happen to them. Next, you have the panelists, experts on this particular experience that they have never even thought about, not to mention having experienced, introducing fragments from their inner visions, and before the dissection is complete, the fiber of the moment is tied into a knot. And you know what, we do this every day and not even realize it. Translation—we cannot live outside of ourselves; few of us even realize there is an outside to ourselves. If you can't explain it in a language or think about it in a language, then it deserves no credence. The alphabet creates yet another box to climb out from. Clearly this reflects inadequacies often overlooked in our attempts to interpret and understand the natural world in which we live. Oftentimes it's not even a word to describe but something much deeper, a feeling that resonates from deep within the bowels of the human experience, wearing no particular face, hat, or shoes, only a feeling, an energy that speaks to your heart and smiles. Many of the gifts and blessings are missed because the world becomes very noisy. The quiet, soft voices from within simply cannot compete with such a noisy world. Let's challenge ourselves to be our own best friend and recognize the cries, laughter, and lessons that so ever softly arise from within. In all our hearts lie all the answers we seek. After all, the heartbeat in which we all enjoy today was relayed through birth from the dawn of time.

LET US ALL PREPARE TOO

. . . .

(2008)

The rainbow is a spectacular painting of nature requiring cooperation among the atmospheric moisture in concert with rays from heaven. A splendid production provided the observer is positioned to receive; failure of proper position distorts the angles and allows such beauty to go unnoticed. So too is the wisdom of God, shining before us as a lighted beacon attempting to rescue the helpless at sea. Spiritual vision does, however, require preparation as a prerequisite to receive such. A teacup is limited in capacity relative to that of a bucket or pail.

UNDER THE SWEET GUM TREE

. . . .

(Revised on June 17, 2008, and continued on June 25, 2008)

Sitting under the sweet gum tree next to the corner of the road on hot summer days was my favorite pastime. All five—or six-year-olds, each and every day, were loaded with pure magic. I had sufficiently displaced all the vegetation with my Tonka toys and managed to dig holes and miniature tunnels in the soft sandy loam that covered most of the yard, which seemed to be in much greater concentration right where I liked it, underneath the sweet gum tree. Usually I had it all to myself, but I preferred when Marvel Ann would let Wayne come and play or Mrs. Hill would allow Tommy to find his way across the street for a day of digging and taking turns filling buckets of sandy loam and dumping it onto one another's heads while seated on the ground with our eyes clinched tighter than ever.

On occasion my mom would provide us with lunch breaks of lemonade and sandwiches on the patio but sometimes announced that I had to come in for lunch and to take a nap. Boy, there was some crying going on. The kids would sit outside and eagerly await my return to the shade of the sweet gum tree. By the time we were done at the end of the day, we were just filthy, and our mothers didn't hesitate to hose us down outside before extending any invitation to come inside and take a bath. Many times my mom would surprise us all by taking all the neighborhood kids to the community swimming pool at H. B. Pemberton High School. Needless to say, she was truly one of the favorite neighborhood moms that also doubled as the music teacher at M. W. Dogan Elementary School, and being beautiful and talented didn't manage to hurt her stock either. I can hear her now. "Music is a single succession of tones, single or combined." After all this is where I was going to spend my elementary years. All the kids from the neighborhood attended school there, and I certainly couldn't wait until my number came up. Boy, eat, drink, and be merry—Marshall, Texas, in the mid to late-1960s was the bomb.

My father was a policeman. In fact he and Gene Whitaker were the first blacks to join the police force in Marshall in 1958. This was something very special, I knew it then, but my appreciation grew tremendously as I matured. One of the most vivid memories of my father on duty in the police car occurred in the summer of 1968. I had just completed second grade and was carrying out my summer ritual of digging under the sweet gum tree, listening to top ten soul hits of the day. Betty, our neighbor Tommy's older sister, and Wayne's aunt usually played loud music most of the day with the exception of the afternoons until the soaps were done. I loved it, but it annoyed my mom at times. Up drove my father around midmorning. This particular week he was on the day shift, which started at 6:00 a.m. and ended at 2:00 p.m. The patrol car was white but due for a washing as a result of several days of earlier rains, and by now the red clay was unforgiving. The blue square background on the side of the front doors that displayed the Marshall Police logo was almost completely covered with red clay, Marshalls trademark. He looked down at his lap and then raised up one of the most adorable German shepherd puppies I had ever seen, six weeks old and dressed out in a black jacket with silver accents. Champ, he was called. He was a loyal friend for life. The elders always said that a good dog would walk quietly at its owner's heels, which defined Champ precisely, all instinct, without any formal training. Up until I left home for college, we were inseparable. Champ was the man. I also loved to ride around in the police car and talk on the external microphone to my friends in the neighborhood, but the sudden whistle of the siren and flash of the emergency lights would excite every youngster within hearing distance. Here they would come, running from all directions and all sizes with and without shoes. "Mr. Williams and the police car is here!" "Do it again, and again, and again, Mr. Williams, thanks so much!" Teeth were bared on every face. This literally made our day and held us over until the snow-cone man showed up late in the evening. I liked coconut, Reggie would get strawberry, and Wayne liked grape. Then quickly back under the sweet gum tree, we would return to recline and enjoy our treat.

Our family was held in such high esteem throughout the community. My mother, the beautiful, talented music teacher, was loved by all and one of Marshall's favorite sons—"Big Brother," "Big," "Twin," or "Al," as most knew him. And Daddy to me, as one of Marshall's first policemen of color—what a work of art. And they both belonged to the community, never once embracing airs of "I'm better than you" or "I look down on you" but quite the opposite, and everyone knew this.

Summer days were long in those days. Summertime itself lasted at least half of a year. The heat of the sun would sting your skin as would a preheated oven awaiting a Thanksgiving turkey. Tonka toys soon became minibikes and minimotorcycles, the backyard doubled as a football field or basketball court, depending on the season, and my six-week-old puppy has become a young man. I tied him underneath

the apple tree my grandfather planted prior to his death. The dog chain over time fashioned the perfect grassless area for spectacular marble games that now has reached legendary status, and I still have the trash can full of winnings to prove it: crystals, bumblebees, cat eyes, toys, boulders, peewees, and so on. My mother loved that tree as well as the other two peach trees he planted there adjacent. When I was young and misbehaving, she would always tell me she would see Big Daddy out under the trees at night and scare me into bed. Big Daddy died when I was in my second year of life. However, my entire life I have felt that I have had a relationship with him. Stories and descriptions of his life's relationships reveal on canvas an image of an unselfish, responsible, quiet, strong, determined, live-and-let-live individual, fully supportive of his twin sons, daughters, and wife, my grandmother. Born 1901 in an area of Harrison County, Texas, known as Gainesville, he attended Marshall public schools and upon graduation joined his father as a lumberjack at Texas and Pacific Railroad station. He made a career of it and upon his father's death replaced him as shop foreman, missing only four days of work in over forty-two years of service. His father held this position as the first black in the early 1900s, he the second.

When putting in perspective the danger involved and the mood of the country at the time my father joined the police force, wow, what ambition and courage. I remember many of the stories my father shared over the years concerning the challenges he faced as a citizen, man, and black policeman on the force. In 1958, when he first joined the force he literally could only discipline people of color. Writing tickets or accosting someone white was prohibited. He would have to call for white backup officers, and the closest would respond to carry on. Or while on duty and in uniform, he literally had the keys to the city. However, in civilian clothes, there were downtown stores he could not frequent. Woolworth, for example, would suddenly have a severe case of amnesia and dismiss all the good deeds he performed—from returning stolen items retrieved from shoplifters to accosting would-be intruders wearing masks. The order of the day somehow managed to prevail. Also, all too often when white officers were in pursuit of someone black, racial epitaphs would spill over the airway on their closed-circuit police radios: "Get that nigger." "Got me a nigger." "Where did that nigger go?" This would happen over and over again and infuriate him to no end. However, he would let it be known. Bill Odom was the chief of police at that time and shared a great deal of affection for my father. He recognized the challenges he faced and admired how he handled such indignities with such dignity. Many of the officers that committed these offenses initially refused to apologize. However, over time and with such increasing respect for my father, there came a time when those same officers would rather shoot themselves in the foot than stand or allow anyone else to stand on the foot of Alphonza Williams.

He ultimately graduated through the ranks to serve as the first black sergeant and detective in 1967 and 1970, respectively, before leaving the force to attend law school at Texas Southern University's Thurgood Marshall School of Law in the fall of 1973. Probably the most challenging times as a police officer occurred in the mid-1960s. The national civil rights movement was in full swing, and Marshall, the proud mother of several institutions of higher learning, held none any higher in esteem than Wiley College, founded in 1873 for the education of Negroes. Wiley was touted as the oldest black school west of the Mississippi River, and with it comes great accomplishment and stature. Like other college campuses and communities all across America, young blacks of all ages responded to the calls of the land for equality and justice for all. The youth of this community responded as well. Sit-ins and rioting were common. Certainly such behavior required police intervention. My father was torn between the two worlds, how to separate the human from the human experience, recognizing the obvious need for change versus the sworn oath and commitment to uphold the law. Many times he would return to the city jail with his patrol car full of protesting college students. I later learned he had many talks with the arrested students while handcuffed and riding in the backseat of his patrol car, and his message was clear: "You guys are doing the right thing, keep doing what you are doing. I'm just doing my job but just keep doing what you are doing. Change has to come. I do applaud your efforts." He did, however, discourage violence. To this day, many of those accounts have come full circle, grown legs and arms right there before me, and spoken loudly about those experiences and how it shaped and molded their approach to conflict in their lives since those days forward.

Now on the other hand as a policeman, my father actually got to do something legally that he enjoyed very much—driving fast cars at high rates of speed. The stories I've heard over the years about he and his brother, Alonza, and their escapades behind the wheel are legendary. They have had a lifetime relationship with motor vehicles. In fact, at birth in September 1933, their parents owned a black four-door 1928 A Model Ford as one of only a few black families in Marshall that even owned a car. That list also includes many of the professors at Wiley and Bishop Colleges. While still little boys, their father would allow them to take turns sitting in his lap and steer the car down the road. The year 1936 brought about a 1932 black four-door Chevrolet, 1940 a 1936 black four-door Plymouth, finally culminating in a brand-new 1949 black Mercury while sophomores in high school. To top it off, Big Daddy's desire to relieve the competition for the Mercury played to their advantage, equaling a second vehicle, a 1933 black four-door Chevrolet. "Now, big man and little man, this one is for you." That response alone could just about tell you how this whole scenario played out. The brand-new black Mercury saw as much of Pemberton High School as did the 1933 Chevrolet. Mind you, this is 1949 in black small-town America, where perhaps two to three families in the entire school were blessed with a family car, not to mention leisure vehicles for the kids, when teachers didn't even drive. Eyewitnesses to this day continue to hold these events in very high esteem, readily sharing memories that have long passed yet still alive. Ready access to such fine machinery all their lives of course created somewhat of careless attitudes regarding vehicles and especially theirs. I remember one story in which Alonza was dropped off to play football, leaving C. J., their first cousin who couldn't drive, to drive while my dad pursued other interest with an attractive young lady in the backseat while speeding down a dark country road. C. J., deficient as he was behind the wheel, couldn't keep his eager eyes on the road and somehow managed to turn over the 1949 black Mercury, necessitating ER visits for all involved. Everyone was scared to death, not of the police but of Big Daddy, and tearfully awaited his arrival to Marshall Memorial Hospital. Surprising to all, he only had one question for the ER doctor upon his arrival, "Doctor, is my son and nephew okay?" The doctor replied, "They're going to be just fine, Mr. Williams." He simply turned and headed out the door, never investigated or inquired as to the condition of the brand-new car that had just been turned over by an unauthorized driver. This incident merely turned into vapor and disappeared, never being mentioned again. Oftentimes than not, they would ride through the streets of Sunny South in search of a worthy street football game to only have the players throw two or three passes, then retreat on a knee to marvel at such an uncommon sight. Alonza would often get mad because he just wanted to play football. My dad, being the voice of reason, helped his brother to appreciate the moment.

Dear, my grandmother would dress these guys just alike from birth, which they continued until the age of twenty-two, and I mean identical down to their shoes and socks. What's funny is male jealousy and competition, being what it is and was. Most guys envied these—owning your own car having, two tall, dark, and handsome fellas to no end, and swearing they had all the girls. The truth was, sure, female advances were made on a daily basis, but they were so bashful and shy neither had the nerve to entertain these advances until their later years of high school. In fact, many of the high school girls would wait for their morning arrival for class just to see how they were dressed and form a long line and force them to walk before them to reach their destination. The college girls, on the other hand, were a bit more aggressive, especially if they parked in front of the Wiley Wildcat Inn and walked less than a block to school. When they would return for lunch or at the end of the day, their car would have young ladies' names written all over the windshield with accompanying phone numbers in white shoe polish. Alonza later related how they were so nervous they would almost pass out. "But no one else knew it but us."

Stories of childhood and young adulthood are laden with a myriad of indelible impressions that we all carry so close to our hearts. The reality that this cycle—birth, copulation, and death—presents and runs its course over and over again like forever-changing seasons is a beautiful thing. Listen to your favorite tunes and sink into a comfortable overstuffed chair that reclines or rocks. With free minds and full hearts, we travel back to that safe place in our lives, surrounded by special people and special times. This is simply magic.

Also during the fall of 1968, I had my first vicarious peek into the college experience by way of my first cousin moving to Marshall to attend Wiley. Boy, this was an exciting time in my life. Louella was the second child of my mom's sister and one of my favorite aunts and uncles, Minnie and Louise Gill. She was big sister, and oh, was she beautiful. It didn't take her long to find her niche or a date. Two events during her tenure at Wiley remain with me to this day: dating and eventually marrying Ronald Charles and pledging AKA. Ronald was a tall, fair-skinned fella with light-colored eyes that matched his hair that happened to be quite an athlete. He was the captain of the baseball team and a pitcher with such a toss that it earned him professional consideration. It also didn't hurt that his father was one of only two black doctors in our community. I remember many a day when Lou and Ronald would come to visit. How much fun we had just throwing the football in the backyard and going out for passes. Because at that time in my life, I was determined to play professional football, and no one could convince me otherwise. Homer Jones wore number 45 for the New York Giants and Otto Love 00 for the Wiley Wildcats, they both were my idols. Homer Jones married Sue McDonald, a lady that lived one block from where I was raised, and offered me the opportunity to meet a real-life professional football player at the ripe old age of eight or nine years old right there in Marshall. Wiley's football program was in its twilight years. I do remember, however, a homecoming game probably in 1969 or 1970 where Lou and Ronald arranged for me to meet number "00" Otto Love. I think his name and the number on his jersey blew me away, but as a young fan of the Wildcats football team and a future professional football player, I thought he was pretty cool. Lou and Ronald did surprise me with an exceptional gift for my ninth birthday. I was playing football in the backyard, emulating Homer Jones if receiving or Otto Love if a running back, on the eleventh day of December 1968. My fingers were nearly frostbitten and my cheeks were ruby red from the constant cool, dry, late-autumn, early-winter resistance I parted as I ran up and down the imaginary sidelines with time running out, scoring multiple unopposed touchdowns.

Up drove Lou and Ronald in the Cougar. It was green with a half-vinyl black top, and they had a large flat box on their lap. Immediately, I thought, "This can't be what I think it is." As they got out of the car, Lou accidentally spilled a root beer float onto a black-and-white dress she was wearing that was designed and sewn by our grandmother. Busy trying to camouflage my gift, she lost the recollection that the topless drink was barely hanging on the edge of the dashboard and an unexpected nudge with her elbow caused it to topple over and spill on her dress. This was not the time of year to stand around and wait for it to dry, so she hurried into the house for relief and left Ronald with the task of removing this large flat box that was covered only with a brown paper bag. I couldn't believe my eyes. It was what I had been worrying my mom and dad about for months, an electric football set, one of the first versions with plastic yellow and white men that allowed you to apply to them your own numbers.

Aside from Louella, Ronald had one other masterpiece worth mentioning, the Roach. The Roach was a 1962 white Plymouth Coupe given to him by his father that he broke down and rebuilt into a puke-green stallion with burgundy interior, jacked up on mag wheels, and under the hood was a smooth-running big-block muscle engine. Time and time again I would ask him to take me with him over to Denson's Garage as he monitored the progress of the rebuild. Upon returning home, my mom would make us both remove our shoes at the door to avoid tracking onto her freshly mopped floor. The thin layer of oil and sand had collected in the threads of our shoes because, after all, this was an automobile repair shop in all its glory.

To this day, this car represents one of the most unique muscle cars I had ever seen. Riding around in the front seat, listening to the tunes of the day, mainly Motown and its perfection, made me feel like a "big boy" and further whetted my appetite for young-adult college life. Louella, on the other hand, visited my mom quite frequently to keep her abreast of her progress in school and just the overall college scene. I, on the other hand, was front and center, taking it all in. I will never forget the fall of 1969 that was the first semester of her second year when she decided to pledge AKA. I can still recall the meetings she and her line sisters would have at our house to hide from their big sisters and prepare for upcoming Greek shows, which included a balance of new choreographed steps with popular tasteful songs of the day. My mom, with her background in music, served as the perfect critic. The duet "I'm Gonna Make You Love Me" by Diana Ross and the Supremes and the Temptations to this day recreates a typical rehearsal evening complete with singing and dancing, with the added attraction of my most and best thing of all, chocolate-chip cookies hot out of the oven, accompanied by a tall glass of milk. Somehow the fall of the year just makes some things better, especially this treat. Our living room was split level, and the split naturally served as the stage. Lou had a beautiful voice. She was Dianna Ross, and two other girls were the Supremes. There was one Supreme I just couldn't get over and simply adored, Mary Ann, from Houston, Texas. In my mind's eye, I can still see her smile with that 1960s Dianna Ross flip up hairdo and a voice to match.

Black Beauty was a childhood book I had read, or at this age, should I say, only two or three years prior. *Black Beauty* had a companion throughout the story by the name of Mary Ann; she was a shetterling pony, short, sassy, and cute, clearly one of my favorite characters in this story. Every time

I would see Mary Ann or hear her name spoken, my heart would fill with an emotional glow just as it did for Black Beauty's friend, Mary Ann. I guess this can be described as my first crush.

Standing all nine or ten years old, I finally had to accept the fact that I was just too short. Among all my friends, I was constantly reminded of the enviable position I was in and loved every minute of it. My buddies would come by just to peek through the window and get a glimpse of these girls doing their thing. By the end of pledge season, we were all experiencing varying degrees of withdrawal. All we had left now was the *Righteous Russell Show* on 1450 KMHT Radio Marshall from 7:00 p.m. to 10:00 p.m. Monday through Friday, and at best, this was a distant second .

However, soon thereafter, Righteous Russell gradutated from small town KMHT radio Marshall to the big city microphone of KOKA in Shreveport, Louisinana, just some thirty miles east of Marshall. I recall hearing that same old high energy voice emitting from a different location of the radio dial, even though I was only eleven or twelve I recall being really proud of him on his move up. Russell happened to be a distant cousin of ours and in some respects my father treated him like a little brother. I recall them sitting at the kitchen table, that doubled as my dads office, so he thought but my mom was not having it, on numerous occassions as my father offered advice and support to this young talent.

One event that continues to measure as one of my foundest memories of childhood is the evening I shared with the Jackson 5. By the time I reached the sixth grade J5 had been out about two years. In fact I recall like yesterday hearing "I want you back" for the first time. It was the fall of 1969, probably October, while waiting in a long line to get a haircut at Mr. Clarks. His barber shop was on the side of his house just a couple of blocks away. Every evening, except Sunday and Monday, boys of all ages would fill the side yard and play basketball or football until their number would come up for the chair. This particular east texas fall evening, the crispness was sharp and the evening sun was a clumsy orange against a beautiful blue sky. I distinctly recall Ricky, Mr. Clarks middle son who happened to be about three years my senior, walking out onto their front porch and motioning to me to come see. He said, "Kirk I want you to come hear this little boy sing, you all are about the same age". And I replied, "is he in the house"? He said "no, it's a record". It completely caught me off guard because up until this point in my life I had never heard of kids singing on records, ever, I walked up the stairs went into the living room and had a seat. I even still remember the brown fabric of the living room sofa and chair glissening in response to the evening rays from an uncovered window. Ricky walked over to the record player and put the needle to the vinyl and there it was, I couldn't believe my ears. I had him replay that song over and over again until my turn came up for the chair. As soon as I got home I started my campaign for this new Jackson 5 record that I had to have, I couldn't believe a little boy was not only singing on a record but jamming too, that was unreal.

Nevertheless, later in the spring of 1972, the Jackson 5 was on tour and coming to Shreveport for the first time. As luck would have it, guess what young, upcoming, radio personality would be their host and chauffer for the evening, Russell Timmons, better know as Righteous Russell, my cousin. Russell made the call to my Dad, "hey Al check and see if Kirk wants to see the Jackson 5 when they come to town, I'll have them the entire evening, in fact you and Laura should also come and hang out with their parents". Before my Dad could finish the question I was jumping for joy, it was a done deal.

We met them at the Howard Johnsons Motel on Interstate-20, hours before the concert, played cards, listened to music, snacked and talked. I recalled how calm I was and how delightful and nice these guys were, Jermaine was the most talkative and we all seemed to get along just fine. I remembered asking a dumb question after sitting around for a while listening to music. I think we were playing cards in Jermaines room. I recall he already had his 8-track or cassette player set up, complete with wall mounted speakers above the door and on the wall listening to some pretty good tunes, of which I had never heard and I asked the question to the effect of if that was another artist, he looked at me kinda crazy and responded, "no thats me", how embarrissing. My parents even hit it off with their parents, so much so that we were invited to Los Angeles to visit them there as well. The concert was spectacular, I couldn't believe these were the same guys I had just played cards, snacked and talked with, truly unbelievable, especially for a twelve year old from Marshall, Texas, this was too much.

Back to the motel after the concert, my parents and I went in to say goodbye and thank them for their hospitality and kindness. By this time they had all showered and were getting ready for bed, I remember Michael with his PJ's on peeping under the curtains downstairs onto the parking lot at a few fans that had discovered their location. I really didn't know how to ask for an autograph. It was hard for me to concieve of asking kids, my age and a little bit older for an autograph. But Mrs. Jackson was apparently in tune with my struggle and grabbed the folded Howard Johnson advertisement from the end table, laid it open and had each one of her sons to sign it for me. The only son she couldn't find at that moment was Tito, even Randy signed as his mom spelled out his name for him, as he was quite young during this time. And as a show of affection, Mrs. Jackson and the boys extended us an invitation to visit the family in Los Angeles, Jermaine wrote down their home address and phone number at his mothers request, thank you again Mrs. Jackson.

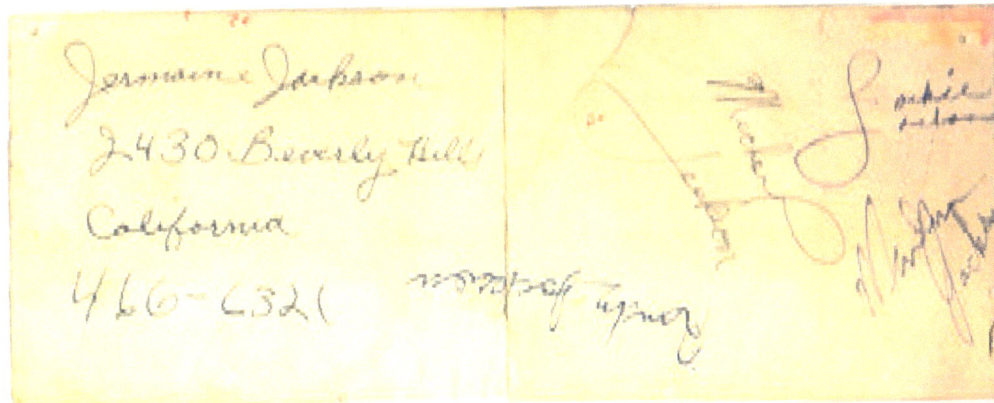

MESSAGE TO MY SONS

(March 20, 2013)

Hey, guys, I'm very proud of you all and love you very much, you have no idea. As your experience in life lengthens, so too will your understanding as young men. I've been there and done that; it's nature's design. With time, your reach for greatness will consume you, for that is your bloodline. The frauds of society will become so ever apparent to the point of confusing you if you are not soundly anchored by truth. Have the courage to trust your heart, for the truth and what we all have been socialized to believe are often dissimilar. That too poses a significant hurdle, but your bloodline provides the necessary ingredients for lift. Most of these waters you will have to navigate on your own and find peace within yourself; it's called maturation. At its endpoint, as men, we will find ourselves nearly on the same page. My father, your grandfather, spoke these prophetic words to his son when I was near your ages, and I couldn't see that far at that time. With continued inner travels, experience, and further acquaintance with oneself, it's all there. All that you are and will be occurred at conception as the rest of your life unfolds, you are just in search of yourself and ultimately your Maker. Peace.

GONE BUT NOT FORGOTTEN

ALPHONZA WILLIAMS
(TWIN)
SEPTEMBER 10 1933
SEPTEMBER 8 1997

Happy Eightieth Birthday, Dad

• •

9-10-2013

Seventeen Years have now passed since we last spoke, though your presence remains, often present when important decisions are made and frequently a sunny-day companion of an evening ride. The memories prevail. Your grandsons, however, young when you last spoke, continue that reach for greatness with the same zest and zeal. Thankfully too, favor continues to reward their efforts. The cliché, "We stand on the shoulders of those that have come before us" rings ever so clear as your, my, and our lifecycle follows its continuum. Kirk II will finish the University of St. Thomas this year with a BA in Political Science and aspirations to attend Law school. Austin recently graduated in Biochemistry from Rice University and now just completed his first year of medical school at Baylor College of Medicine. Alexander, right on his heels, is also an aspiring doctor, having just completed his second year at Northeastern University in Boston, Massachusetts; Also a Biochemistry major, he was selected through a highly competitive process to spend this semester researching at Harvard Medical School in a Neuroscience Lab, Hopefully one step closer to his goal of attending Harvard Medical School in eighteen months. Baby boy, Adam, just finished High school with numerous accolades, one of which was recognition for perfect scores on the Mathematics and Science sections of the Act College Admissions test. He chose Engineering/Physics as his area of interest and received nearly a full academic scholarship to attend Carnegie Mellon University in Pittsburgh, Pennsylvania. As before, we love you, we miss you, and we remain your pupils.

Your son,

A. Kirk Williams, MD

........as proud as I am of my sons, I am but half the equation, for God has spoken

the other half, as beautiful in as she is out, Margaret Lang-Williams MD

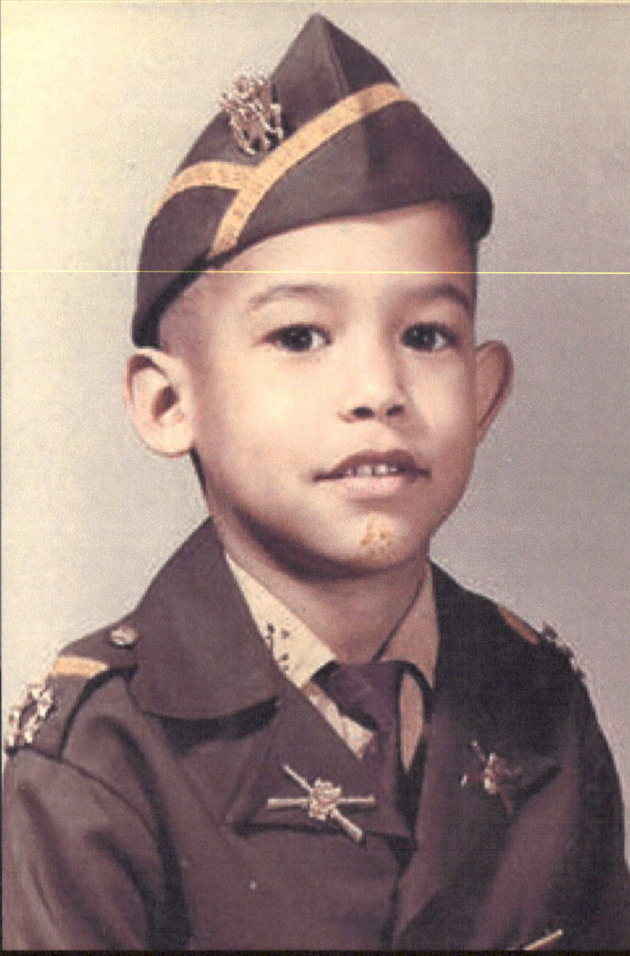

If Only I Knew

•••••••••••••••••••••••••••••

(Winter 2013)

"If only I knew, if only I knew years ago what I know today" is a commonly shared sentiment by those that have traveled the distance and now are nursing ailing feet.

Those that have traveled the distance survived the challenges of matriculation at all levels; indeed, there lies a body of wisdom.

Matriculated into the consciousness and understanding of the is. Truth that speaks to our frailty, vulnerability even insignificance as a citizen of the world body. How then do we convey what's to come to those that have yet to come?

The human spirit is forever changing as our stay here lengthens as we say, "Your priorities will change as your time lengthens here, young one." No, they will evolve in many different wave forms of changing amplitudes and frequencies only to reach that exact place in time, perhaps at different times, though that same place in time. Where your mental, emotional, and spiritual dimensions will slowly give way to a molded, refined existence likened to that of our Maker.

So the challenge remains. How then do we shape, mold, and prepare the yet to come? As they live inside of a song not yet complete, hollowed by an arrangement devoid of the full array of strings, woodwinds, and brass, all of which are accompanied by limited percussion, completely unaware the volume of the full orchestra has yet to play. Yet they know not; they know only what they know as it represents all that is, and in their minds, there is no other. How then do we provide footing for the inevitably compromised?

Their Maker has accounted for such and in fact designed a cloud of tolerance that releases refreshing beads of wet as needed to cleanse their faces of heartache as it polices the boundaries of acceptable, crossed only with consequence.

Provide the dry cotton swath that dries their wet faces and tearing eyes as this too serves as affirmation to his end that is too yet to come.

How the West Was Won

●●●●●●●●●●●●●●●●●●●●●●●●●●●●●

(December 31, 2013)

The Great American West provided many of the very first fictional characters I recall embracing as a child. Local television stations as they were in the late 1960s and early 1970s numbered 3 in my neck of the woods of small-town America: NBC, ABC, and CBS. Cherish I did were those Friday and Saturday night flicks of *Cowboys and Injuns*, weekdays with Clint Eastwood as Rowdy of Rawhide; Clayton Moore as the Lone Ranger, with his trusted sidekick Tonto, played by Jay Silverheels; Roy Rogers; Matt Dillon in *Gunsmoke*; Chuck Connors as the Rifleman; and so on, but Stoney Burke was my mostest and bestest favorite character. So much so I wore a Stoney Burke get-up for my kindergarten school photos. I recall a black cowboy hat with a red shirt outlined with white embroidery, Western fashioned, on both fronts and around the collar, blue jeans and kicker boots down to and including imitation spurs and a six-shooter tied down on my right hip. It takes my mom to talk about that black felt cowboy hat I was so proud of. As she tells the story, I only took that hat off to take a bath, which I hated, and to sleep. In fact, she relates I wore that cowboy hat until it became a sombrero, trading its cowboy curls on both sides for the fallen, flat, rounded look.

Now get this. I was scared to death of riding a real horse then and now, go figure. But I also remembered my preoccupation with "Gittin' all them damn Injuns." Of course, I didn't say that at kindergarten age, but my intensity mirrored that. They were savages and beyond a nuisance for the wagon trains expanding west. Hurry, cavalry, to rescue the settlers from those savage redskins. Crazy Horse, Red Cloud, Geronimo, and the greatest chief of all, Sitting Bull, with their bows and arrows and sharp knives for scalping, impeded westward progress, according to General George Armstrong Custer, and must be eliminated at once.

Long before studying any US history or having any clue regarding the ways of the world, talking about brainwashing, or more formally, socialization, I was sold. Now, however, as I always try to teach my sons as well as others, things are never as they appear. There are at least two sides to every story, if not more. The *Cowboys and Injuns* wars were really about Native Americans, the original Americans, attempting to preserve, among other things, their real estate holdings and their way of life as it was being stripped from them at will. Outnumbered and centuries behind the military technology curve, they stood very little chance of surviving despite true bravery and gallant efforts—warriors to the end. They did eventually succumb. Though, It wasn't just smallpox, or the brute might of the cavalry, or the destructive power of the cannon or the Gatling guns shearing of flesh that proved to be most lethal.

It was the tool consistently used over and over again throughout history that proved to be the most effective of all—the fork tongue. As the Indians say, if you have watched any old Cowboys and Injuns flick, you've heard this as well: "Um Pale Face Speakum with a Fork Tongue."

From promises made to Geronimo to return to his homeland after a brief stay in Florida, to numerous peace treatises guaranteeing residual reservation land, only to be significantly whittled away over time to only a fraction of its original size, until eventually nothing. This too was reflected in President Andrew Johnson's failure to honor the freed slaves with forty acres and a mule as promised. Nevertheless, the Indians were so often referred to as savages that lacked worship. Sitting Bull made a profound statement that still lives today. In the archives is a picture of Sitting Bull seated, legs crossed, on the ground before an accumulation of buffalo bones stacked by the US Cavalry to over fifteen to twenty feet at its apex as he stated, "And they call us savages."

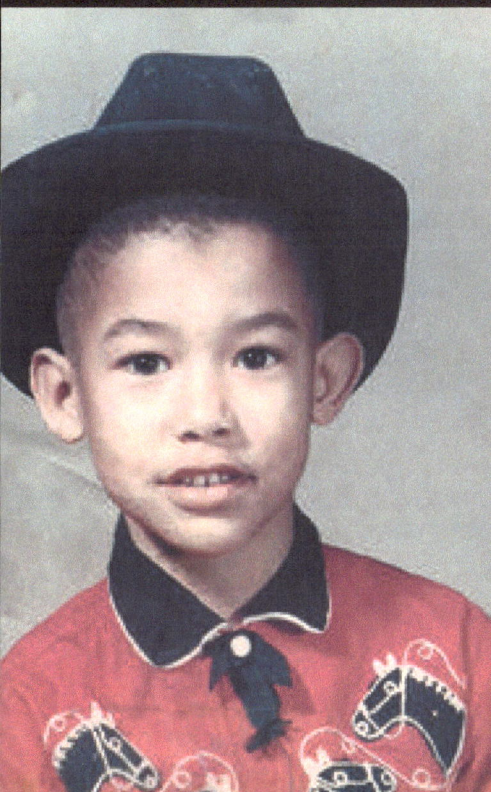

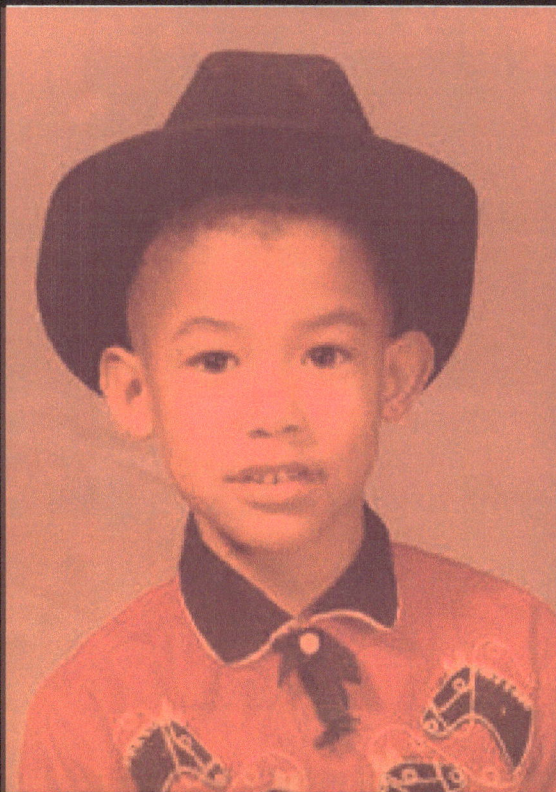

ADDICTIONS OF THE WEST

• •

(January 13, 2014)

The classrooms of medicine, religion, nature, etc., as a matter of theory, will teach and cite evidence of moderation as a means to all-around good mental, emotional, spiritual, and physical health. Addictions of the West, however, blur the lines of balance and excess as the latter prevails. Left unchecked, this allows the human condition to flourish and unfortunately tips the axis of balance to its detriment. The underlying pursuit is motivated by greed and material wealth above all else. Attempting to isolate oneself from temptation assumes that willpower is a switch of leisure. Even among the most disciplined of authors, this remains a clumsy task at best. You see, even the best of intentions are still rooted in the soil of greed. Kind of like the shifting sand beneath your feet as the tide retreats, stable only in its absence. However, recognizing that the soul of man is already sanctioned by God, man's demand of it, and the labeling of God's order as unnatural or wrong remains a forest; it is man's demands that are unnatural and contrary. It should not be the ability of congress to sanction and demand that the will of our Maker be a crime against that that it has created, because our wishes and addictions are contrary. As the governing body of the land, its compass must remain true to the earth's magnetic field. Otherwise, our course is veered in the direction that is not true and, as consequence, not rewarded by his favor.

And What You Think You Are Seeing Is What You Are Seeing

••••••••••••••••••••••••••••••

(2008)

It's obvious that one is forced to think for him or herself, there is not a chance of ever receiving accurate information through the media or governmental bodies, for their agenda are targeted for the few at the expense of many. Just this year, the Bush administration was forced by a federal judge to release documents acknowledging the effects of global warming that was compiled by our own government; yet he consistently denied its existence. This information was scheduled for release in 2004 but was suppressed by his administration since that time. If such gross negligence occurred in the private sector, it would be defined as criminal when taking into consideration all the potential injury that was and will occur as a result of such irresponsible behavior. Shortly thereafter, in the spring of 2008, congress voted down a global warming bill that would have placed some stipulations on industry in an effort to curb these adverse outcomes, and they rationalized it as "bad for business." So was the abolishment of the beastly act of slavery, as they also rationilzed it as "bad for business" according to the wealthy plantation owners. They continued to push for their way of life, that was predicated on the indefinite continuation of slavery. This is where statements like "To be on the knowing end of destroying God's creation with such zest and zeal is spiritually ill" comes from. Such discussion is increasingly rejected by modern audiences; nevertheless, it is these very audiences that offer any hopes for resolution.

Sci-Fi

. . . .

(August 2013)

God made us all in a balanced, special way. Our makeups are accompanied by the inherent checks and balances that maintain our mental, emotional, and spiritual foundation. Balanced with a forward lean towards him, yet recent times reflects a different order, leaning away from him. The balance, once consistent in all the world and its people, now behaves to its detriment as the multidimensional once-balanced makeup gives way to an aberration. Organism failure has allowed the dimension of greed to flourish at the expense of all others and things. What change or changes in nature precipitated this disaster? Likened to the effects of a cancer as it grows, sickens, and pains until eventually it kills. What led to such? Who, what, where, and when did this imbalance occur that has now manifest itself as thinning ozone? Much like a failed experiment out of a sci-fi flick—*laboratory organism escapes from lab and transforms us all into unthinking, uncaring, disrespectful beings to all things divine*—attacking the very hand that not only feeds us but also made us. You often hear "Step back" from a situation and take a second look. Participation clouds objectivity, and since most are preoccupied with participation, it would do us all good to chill for a second in an attempt to regain balance. Stop feeding this organism called greed; slow the cancer before it kills us all.

In Pursuit

. . . .

(Summer 2013)

It is common to be preoccupied in this world so big in pursuit of what we think is the answer without ever really knowing the question, accepting it and embracing it as it is passed down from one generation to the next. Just go with the flow, right into a room full of mirrors reflecting that which has no face, shoes, or hat. Blessings are needed to escape the rapid and swift currents, for the bank offers peace—peace away from inaccuracies and untruths we struggle with on a daily basis. We struggle because it's inconsistent with our divineness. Although unable to escape the human condition and addictions of the flesh, spiritually move to the bank and remain a spectator of such foolishness and allow your soul to rest.

Expectations Unmet

. . . .

(Summer 2013)

Your interpretation comes from your experiences and extrapolations drawn from your base of knowledge as it relates to where you are in this world mentally, emotionally, and spiritually. Just because your expectations of what you think the truth "ought to be" are not met doesn't mean it's not true but that that you are disputing may be the truth in its highest form. Einstein was thought to be an idiot, not because he was but because he was misunderstood.

Watch the Spin

. . . .

(December 10, 2013)

Quite simply, truth is fundamental to understanding, and understanding is fundamental to peace. We see it daily as it parades before us, but because of the spin, the spin placed by the larger world that programmed us all to serve it, our confidence shrinks at the very thought of connecting the dots that brings into focus the ultimate blessings. Thinking we have it figured out, going through all the motions of celebrating what we think are great feats, yet remaining empty once it's complete is but confirmation we are amiss. Open the eyes of your heart. However, be constantly aware of the spin; do not allow it to steal your joy and ultimately your peace.

Do Not Overlook

. . . .

(October 5, 2013)

Oddly enough, in our busy lives, often daily the simple things are overlooked. The answers and truths right under our noses are dismissed for the preferred cycle of nonsense we are all caught up in. Simple is wholesome, reinvigorating, and when fully understood and embraced, is the blessings we are all in search of. Most will spend their entire lives in search of that ultimate blessing, which is quite simply *peace*.

Conversations from Time to Time

• •

(Summer 2013)

Conversations from time to time allows the mind and soul to escape, time-travel, and seek refuge from conflicts that ail. Freeze and slow the frames of times now past though very alive. As the lenses of time have sharpened our vision, meaning is now heightened. Outside of uncertainty and truly enjoying the favor of time, the path is clear and broadened. Likened to a motion that is slow, steady, and exact. Connecting the dots in small increments, one at a time, slowly gives way to places and faces of your life. Lessons of wisdom, on and off the chalkboard, resonate as affirmation to these times now past though very alive.

ROOM WITH A VIEW

· ·

(Summer 2013)

Carve out that space between your ears, offering panorama in Technicolor, of which that technology recently developed for consumption, though, forever present in the hearts of men. Although the world and its people are beyond our control, your control, nevertheless, all that matters is how what happens affects you. And how what happens affects you is ultimately rooted in the wisdom of your perspective, foundation in truth, and spiritual bases with its yield. As the architect of that space between your ears, that room with a view offering panorama in Technicolor is but a product of you, the design of which reflects genetic compositions, teachings, and acceptance of truth, if possible, that ultimately yields thy armor. Varied and tested from the villages at dawn to the pyramids of many cultures all while resting on an escalator in Times Square, His resources of wisdom are vast as it is passed from one generation to the next by the pair of twenty-three. All that you are and will be occurred at conception, as your life unfolds, you are simply in search of yourself and ultimately your Maker.

THE SINGLE-HEADED MONSTER

(June 2013)

Sounds a lot like the single-headed monster, the single-headed monster that knows only one end regardless of consequence, that will soon eventual its own demise, that is known to the world as capitalism. It was called into existence some years ago on an experimental basis, had to be, for now it's an experiment gone wrong. At its inception, the concept appealed to a few; those few with the power of the pen that agreed among themselves and pressed on. Was there any due diligence, who cares, the perceived benefit to those few too great and as a consequence still remains without drag enough to slow its destructive swirl. Nearsighted as it was, now blind as can be. What psychological factors allowed perpetuation of such irresponsible behavior as we fill the pews on Sunday mornings in prayer? Are we to police ourselves or continue to bare nature's fury?

CONSERVATIVES AND JESUS

• •

(January 6, 2014)

Over the past six or seven years, I have paid more attention to the cable news stations than ever before, partly a function of getting older as I warn my sons their day too is coming; the other, however, is an attempt to stay abreast of the daily political rub as so often it changes. My brother from another mother, residing in the White House as one of the most powerful persons on the planet, is *waaaay* too much for most to handle. This has precipitated feelings, ideas, and thoughts usually less obvious but now bulging as most can't help themselves, pushed smooth over the edge and unashamedly taking aim and stripped of their masterful layers of deception and now naked, exposing their true feelings, so take note. But I recall a discussion sometime ago that broached the question as to if Jesus were here in the flesh, what would he be, a liberal or a conservative? I'm like "Really"; is there any question about that? He was born out of the yearning of his people, the oppressed, for salvation doesn't sound much like those of privilege. Without getting bogged down in history, facts, and inconsequential debate not readily available or known by the simplest of men, the truth belongs as much to him as it does the privileged; it belongs to no one earthly being or groups but shared equally by all. Most discussions and opinions valued are by those that have studied who knows what and are celebrated in our society for who knows why, though the accomplished. But where I'm from, the textbook of life is an even greater teacher, and the old folks better students. You see, old folks from my neck of the woods that sit on the porch in the evenings and spit are no different than those of other places, especially those with little education and even fewer worldly possessions can hold court daily, never repeating a single lesson in truth, for they know many. Their wisdom reflects the earth as you can feel their hearts as they ache and see the fresh footprints of truth in the soft sand beneath their bare feet. If I were a betting man, and I am, this is where my loyalties would lie.

A Conversation with Time

· ·

(February 4, 2014)

It's a difficult task to look forward attempting to fix your life without all the variables at your disposal as many are physiological, others psychological, often not even knowing that it is impossible to have them all or at least most of them until well into the later decades of life—and that's only if you are willing to respond by following the roads less traveled along the way. From where you sit as you read this article, look around; you can only see what you can see based on your location and position; make a mental note. Now get up and move five feet to the left or right and five steps forward from there—what do you see different? And I'm not talking just big but small as well. Now go outside and take notes while looking north, then south, seeing something completely different. However, in every position, you are certain what you are seeing. If nothing changes, all is good, but there lies the problem. Life is like the changing of positions, as your own mental, emotional, and spiritual chemistries by design will change over time, offering a different focus or vantage point to see things that previously were concealed. This exercise is known as maturation. Every new variable is like a cog in the wheel that alters expectations and desires from that point forward. Previous wants are now slightly different, and multiple cycles of such will widen the gap even further. So any attempt to fix or freeze any of these above frames is but an impossibility. We are designed to grow in all dimensions of our lives, and growth by definition is change. Nevertheless, driven by the multiple insecurities that we all face, our tendency is in that direction. So the youths of the world are especially challenged in making long-term goals and following through.

As they decide as a grade schooler or teenager to pursue one area of interest, once through puberty and into young adulthood, their internal environments may now offer a different flavor, and another five to ten years still, another taste develops. That's where sayings like "Listen to the old folks, for they didn't get to be old and stupid" comes from. Common mistakes that we all make through our evolution are to assume that the present conditions that we feel so confident about will always be. If so, taking a stance and defending it with all your might and will, up to and including burning bridges, would be worth the gamble. However, knowing that change is to come as it represents one of the many constants in the universe renders such efforts futile.

My approach, which I realize now, was not all my own doing but a blessing in that I always had an affinity for the old folks, I guess, in a way, using their experiences as that hindsight that obviously eludes one until later in life. For this I'm sure serves as an advantage for those with the presence of mind to listen to and follow instructions. They unashamedly shared many mistakes they made along the way and likewise shared positive, encouraging words reflecting their experiences, hoping to strengthen and help those that would come behind them, to avoid unnecessary trials and tribulations. Stressing "no need to reinvent the wheel"; life is way too short. Some mistakes can be avoided. Save your time and energy for those specific to you that are unavoidable, overall these experiences did and still do prove to be beneficial. Listening to stories day in and day out about trials and tribulations over their years and somehow managed to capture as much wisdom as possible to store for my times to come. Often seated at the feet of my parents, grandparents, aunts, and uncles, but the sweet stuff, the gravy, was the neighborhood old folks. Ms. Annie would sit on her narrow front porch with steep steps in the evenings, chewing tobacco and spitting. I would sit on the steps with my grade-school back to her, listening to every word she uttered regarding her take on the world as she saw it and what she thought about my dog Champ. I specifically recall sitting under a big shade tree on a midsummer morning, watching Big Daddy, as the neighborhood children called him, clean his morning catch of a big turtle and bucket full of fish. Somehow the conversation turned to my grandfather, Telas Williams, who had died when I was only two years of age, as he and Big Daddy were friends. His account and message regarding Telas Williams's greatness on that midsummer morning provided me with a link to my Y chromosome that I felt then, while still in grade school, and now as an adult. Or I took notes while enjoying conversations with Ms. Hill, Ms. Boots, and Pops, or Pawpaw, whose favorite seat was on a bench beneath the huge oak tree. All the above, whose participation represents the village, as some of the many teachers whose wisdom somehow played a role in my mental, emotional, and spiritual development. Reminding us all that truth has no face, price, or preference as it is available and plentiful to all that seek it.

Time and time again, in raising my kids, I would try and keep lessons in front of them, on the chalkboard. Objectively, I hoped to buffer the subjective changes that were soon to come as I warned them their internal environments would take on a new flavor. Puberty is one of the first challenges as the body's hormonal roller coaster is unleashed, feeling and thinking different for the first time. My efforts revolved around education of this process in hopes of providing the necessary tools to work through this maze of temptation and defiance. Regardless of your feelings or thoughts, you magically suddenly think no one else on the planet understands but you. It's not so. The old folks have already been there and done that. You've got to trust someone. Just follow instructions for a year or two until this all subsides. Otherwise, mistakes can be made now that you will spend the rest of your life regretting. Nevertheless, this also applies to all the children of the world, adults too. You are seated temporarily in one place now, but ultimately you will be on the other end of the spectrum, give yourself a chance to maximize the experience that you will enjoy the rest of your life. Although I am certain you are certain that what you feel is real, I am equally certain that what you are now certain of will evolve into many different realizations as time progresses. Use the experience of those that have come before you as a road map to avoid dead ends and wastes of time. It's impossible to move forward when you are constantly taking steps backward or constantly having to recover from setbacks. An intelligent response would be to create a sounding board that could loosely resemble hindsight to benefit you now. Sit at the feet of the old folks and recognize all the intersections as the lines cross, for there lies the answers. Arm yourself with their wisdom, for it is free, accurate, and abundant, for this too they already know.

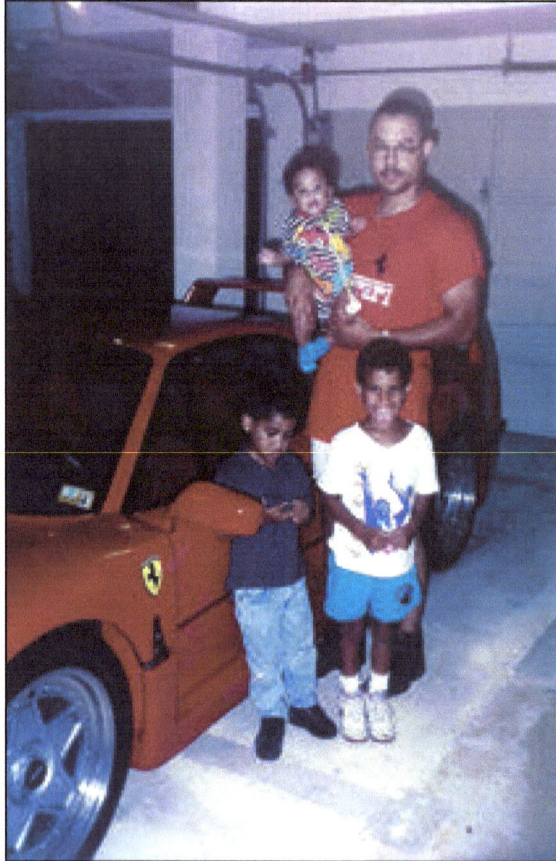

.......Beautiful cars huh? Blessed I was to be able to afford this at an early age, Ferrari F-40, Ferrari 512 TR, Ferrari Testarossa and the Ferrari 328 GT. However, I didn't listen to the old folks, those that had already walked the trail I was about to travel. My father counseled me repeatedly and aggressively for not having greater vision. He had placed a smaller investment before me, 130 acres of what he felt would be a great future oil and gas property that I wasn't feeling. I had to have the multiple Ferrari's, HAD TO HAVE IT, you do the math. And guess what, he was absolutely correct. Nestled along I-20 in the heart of oil and gas country, East Texas, the opportunity existed only because of his relationship with the property owner, all of which I took for granted. I missed it, not being able to see beyond my own biology, and desires of the time, and not fully respecting the wisdom of those that had come before me. I had all of this under control, "Daddy you just don't understand", I was completely wrong, in a very big way.......Listen to those that have come before you, ALWAYS.

FORKS IN THE ROADS

• •

(2008)

I've been waiting for this moment for decades, waiting for inspiration, motivation, or just flat being pushed out of my comfort zone, which yields uneventful, restless days into the current of forever-changing waters that run deep within the hearts of men. The world provides us all with a sounding board to test the many theories we think to be true. Most of which are guided by impulses or even group sessions that the majority will just decide "This is how it is." It has to be true for it is in all the history books and on the news. Who is my heart to question the wisdom of such accomplishment and documentation? I am a single voice in a world that doesn't celebrate my kind; in fact, it is just the opposite. The smile of the Creator was not meant for me but for others. Those that we see in positions of authority that speak and tell us what to think, what to feel, how to feel, what is true, and if you don't believe it, you will be punished, now with jail or later with eternal damnation. Well, hell, I'm convinced. The constitution of a very small child growing up in a world so much bigger than they are doesn't have a choice or chance but to believe. Pavlov conditioned the behavior of dumb animals in days; the bigger whole has conditioned the minds of children of the world for centuries. Though my heart is being tugged constantly in the direction of an unpopular corner or a road less traveled. With confidence only in what I have been taught, the unpopular corners and roads less traveled remain as they are.

MANIPULATION

• •

(2008)

The systems of governing, i.e., those created by man to, in effect, control the masses, for whatever purposes, must be examined, at least some. Keep in mind, the system or network that we live within is governed by decisions made at the round table. Men will collaborate and decide. Never mind that the sun always rises in the east and sets in the west. If you are not careful, even this well-established phenomenon becomes debatable. What happens if everyone at the table just claims to like asparagus? Is this a staple that everyone enjoys? And those deciding, being the experts they are, cannot fathom anyone not sharing the same enthusiasm in which they do. After all, this is a healthy vegetable, and no matter what, everyone should enjoy the nourishment it provides. Following this elaborate explanation as to why this is the product of choice, a little further investigation reveals that most of the panelists making the decisions will directly or indirectly benefit from the popularity of this magnificent vegetable. Honesty and trustworthiness—what is that ? This is an agenda that speaks to the selfish interest of a few at the expense of many. This is the system we are forced to embrace and love; to speak out in any way is unpatriotic or radical on one hand or passionate and concerned on the other, depending on the lens.

Success Rooted in Slavery Shares No Burden?

• •

(January 24, 2014)

What does Lehman Brothers, Aetna, JPMorgan Chase, New York Life Insurance Company, Wachovia Corporation (now owned by Wells Fargo), N M Rothschild and Sons Bank in London, Norfolk Southern, *USA Today*, Fleet Boston, CSX, the Canadian National Railway Company, Brown Brothers Harriman, Brooks Brothers, Barclays, AIG, Tiffany and Company, Bank of America, and others not listed here all have in common with regard to slavery? They represent a few of the industrial giants whose beginnings, to greater and lesser degrees, have roots in slavery. Also note, as most economic models suggest, obviously, these giants didn't operate without a supporting staff or in a vacuum. In fact, they spawned off ancillary support businesses that became industries within themselves, directly benefitting from the success of these icons and indirectly benefitting from the institution of slavery as well. As you can see, this foundation quickly expands. In fact, many authors credit slavery as the economic engine fueling the industrial revolution. For example, many of the financial institutions accepted slaves as collateral to acquire loans and as payment and oftentimes even took possession of them on defaulted loans. Many of the insurance giants insured the lives of slaves. JPMorgan Chase admits accepting thirteen thousand slaves as collateral and took ownership of twelve thousand five hundred when the plantation owners defaulted on loans. New York Life Insurance Company's internal history revealed that three hundred thirty-nine of its first one thousand policies written were on the lives of slaves. The railroad companies would rent slaves to lay rail at embarrassing low rates but unashamedly took full advantage of this cheap labor, two of which was the famous John Henry and Rueben. Brooks Brothers, now known for its expensive suits, got their start by selling slave clothing to slave traders. Tiffany and Company was originally financed by slave-picked cotton. Collectively, these industrial giants benefitting from slavery represent trillions in net worth as their economic impacts have extended well into the twenty-first century, and this list doesn't include the many other now-failed businesses that enjoyed success for some time, just not with the same longevity. And as also noted above, their by-product, ancillary-support businesses became industries within themselves, representing billions in economic value and impact. So, yes, the African has contributed greatly to the, literally, building of this country, just without legal title, yet credited nothing.

Is America, the champion of freedom and equality, but a punch line, or does it apply only to certain people? Immigrants, not even American citizens of non-African descent have entered this country routinely and historically over the years and benefited more from the Africans' work than the African himself, an American citizen. Now to bring these things to light for examination somehow makes one the bad guy, the rebel or radical, but let's just try "It's the truth," and anyone that condones such behavior is the "bad guy." Those knowingly benefitted and benefitting from these fruits of labor that perpetrated these immoral, repugnant frauds against humanity somehow not. Are you serious? Any argument in defense of such behavior collapses on itself. "They don't qualify" or "They don't have the training or experience," always rationalizing why you can only do what you want to do. This is all artificial. You made the rules, you change them. Rationalizing the practice of barbarianism for over four hundred years and proudly accepting its fruit, but now the descendants of those that enriched your lives don't qualify? Sure, maybe most are without your credentials because they were busy working centuries for free, affording you the privilege of school, prosperity, hobnobbing, and networking with others of your kind. "Let's just apologize and not talk about it further. Soon it will blow over. The statutes of limitation have run, so they can't sue us or get anything," said with a snicker as they rush to church on the most segregated day of the week, Sunday mornings , to pray to Jesus, to be like him, never dawning on them that the very one they are praying to is the same one they are acting against. I'm just curious, which Jesus are you praying to? The one that condones this routine, consistent "not my brother's keeper" kind of behavior? Oh, him. Well, he doesn't exist, but Lucifer does, always wanting to be like Jesus but always finding a way to weasel out when the opportunity presents. So just stay home and stop lying to yourselves and everyone around you. You don't want to be like Jesus. You want to be just who you are, without the guilt. If you truly wanted to be like Jesus, you've had nearly two thousand years to do so. With roots clearly in slavery by their own internal documentation, you would think that companies so wealthy and prosperous would make some kind of concessions for those unwilling, forced participants contributing to their success. Ever heard of blood diamonds? This is but the same concept. Even today, black Americans hiring at these companies they help build, without title, find it difficult to secure employment at its highest levels, often giving preference to whites—of course, women, other minorities, and even non-American citizens over blacks. You've found a way to justify doing whatever your nature desired historically, no matter how ill. Now find a way to do the right thing and *truly* gain favor with God.

Frederick Douglass referred to the Willie Lynch method of the making of a slave as a scientific process of man-breaking and slave-making. Willie Lynch was a fairly successful British plantation owner from the West Indies who was invited to the colony of Virginia, which was the first European settlement in the New World preceding the thirteen colonies, in 1712 to teach his methods to slave owners. He specialized in the disenfranchising of the African on all levels to, in effect, create a slave. His methods did prove to be successful and were routinely used throughout the slave era. He stressed, "Keep the body, take the mind," often drawing parallels between the slave and the horse with regard to breaking their will. He also clearly felt a kinship with ancient Rome as he proudly drew parallels between ancient Rome and its use of cords of wood to build crosses for crucifixions versus the colonists' use of the rope for hanging. He all but guaranteed three hundred if not a one thousand years of success if the slave owners would use his methods that he referred to as a "kit." In short, it involved using differences among the slaves and exaggerating them. Use distrust and envy for control purposes. He stated that distrust is stronger than trust and envy stronger than adulation, respect, or admiration, focusing on dismantling the family structure by pitting male against female and female against male, lessening the male's value in the eyes of the female. Break the mother so she will break the offspring in the early years of development. Pit young male against old male and old male against young male, old female against young female and young female against old female, dark against light and light against dark, one language against another, positions of privilege against another—all to, in effect, heighten distrust among the slaves, leaving the overseer as the slaves' confidant. But the ultimate goal was to "put the fear of God in him." This was done, as a matter of principle, by taking the biggest, strongest, defiant male and strip him of all clothing before the other males, females, and children, tar and feather him, tie each leg to a different horse pointed in the opposite directions, set him afire, and whip the horse until they pull him apart while all the other slaves are watching. The next step is to take a bullwhip and beat the remaining male slaves to near death, careful not to kill them because of their future breeding value. As I set describing this barbaric, ungodly, beast-like activity, it causes me to cringe and tear as these images are horrific, yet they found a way to rationalize this treatment and felt no remorse, for it was repeated over and over again throughout the centuries of the storied old South. So this is the slave that did his part in the building of America. He has paid and continues paying tremendous dues yet benefitting none, for this residual sentiment remains in the black community today.

As stated by Frederick Douglass, this was a studied process, as if a science. What's missing is the antidote. In medicine, as with many processes, there are reversals, antidotes, or even as in psychiatry or psychology, group sessions or group therapies are employed in search of hope for restoration. None of which occurred, as the lingering effects of this barbarianism haunts many blacks to this day. All while the critics line up to cite deficiencies in the state of black America from unemployment and teen pregnancies to crime and incarceration. Talk about "Post Traumatic Stress Disorder", think any of these people qualified for such a diagnosis, just the thought of it stresses me out, not to mention living through it for centuries.

The knowledge of history and self was ablated sometime ago and not restored. Yes, its absence does contribute greatly to such, and restoration would all but represent the first steps to correction. So, yes, the residual of the Willie Lynch methods still affect many today. Its benefits enjoyed by the slaveholders, and America for that matter. Now all stand to criticize the very mind-sets that they help to create. Standing in the shadows of industries with unparalleled wealth, much of which was built on the backs of slaves, yet no one assumes any responsibility for their participation, not even the US government whom we all hold an allegiance to. And here, a few years back, upon the election of Barack Obama, the first black president of the United States, wife, Michelle Obama made a comment to the effect that, now she was proud of her country, and the pundits had a field day with that comment. But they haven't been where she has, not even close, yet now an expert on her perspective as they feel her pain, sure. And if she didn't happen to be the first black First Lady, none of the opposing parties' muckrakers would care. They live completely outside of the black experience and could care less about it, but yes, it is a different perspective as it hasn't a choice but to be. If you were black, just in light of this limited discussion, how would you feel? As far less receives much more attention when others are involved.

It always gets me when the pundits attempt to rationalize how America's participation in slavery was but a small percentage when measured against the rest of the world or that Africans also practice slavery or that the slaves were sold to the Europeans by other Africans to, in effect, deflect guilt and responsibility. No, that's not right. They are all guilty and should atone. The Africans' practice of slavery was much like indentured servitude or debt bonding in the rest of the world, where one would work for a finite period of time. Once the agreed debt is paid, he is then free to work on his own but never treated as chattel. The Africans never envisioned the brand of slavery instituted by the Europeans, ever. With only their own experiences to draw from, they hadn't a clue. Some things as simple as an explanation as to where you have been and who you are would go a long way, but no, not even an apology. Most black Americans know no other context for themselves other than as descendants of slaves. No concept of their place in the earth's history as the original man, or the many parallels with Jesus and his enslaved people for he too was of African descent, or even the tangible history of Egypt and its predecessors. Yes, many know the power of the knowledge of history and self. That's why most of it has been removed, destroyed, or simply taken away and credited to others. Hitler certainly did as he deliberately canon-fired the noses off the sphinx and other relics to remove the Negroid-appearing features upon Germany's invasion of Northern Africa, as well as destroyed numerous archives of recorded history, or as Michelangelo depicted in his painting of the European version of the blond–haired, blue-eyed Jesus that is geographically, historically, ethnically, and biblically incorrect, or the popes secretly praying to the black Madonna and Child, as the list of insults and frauds are numerous and multifactorial. Just steal history, and I suppose in their minds, God's will as well, for they care not about his wisdom, only their own.

Prior to Lincoln's assassination on January 15, 1865, General William T. Sherman issued the Special Field Order Number 15, and President Lincoln approved it, which temporarily gave freed slaves forty acres per family tree out of four hundred thousand acres of land to work. The land extended from the Atlantic Coast of South Carolina to Georgia and Florida, thirty miles in, and additionally the Union soldiers donated some of them excess mules for tilling. So this is where "forty acres and a mule" originated. Now try to imagine how different race relations in America would have been provided the freedman had the opportunity to own and work his own land and had the chance to be self-sufficient economically and to build, accrue, and pass on wealth from as far back as the mid to late 1800s. Nevertheless, after Lincoln's assassination, his successor and southern sympathizer, President Andrew Johnson, revoked Sherman's orders, which returned the land ownership to the original owners, and congress bills of inequality that rendered the freed slaves still dependent on the land owners for survival through sharecropping. The black codes and Jim Crow laws further undermined the efforts of the freed slaves. As a result of these setbacks, it wasn't for one hundred years that the Civil Rights Act of 1964 and the Voting Rights Act of 1965 granted blacks civil rights and the right to vote, respectively, followed by affirmative action rulings. Although, I am far from an expert on these types of social matters, it does, however, appear to this author that not near enough restoration has occurred.

It is quite clear that those within our society, the controlling parties are at odds with the very teachings they claim to hold in the highest of esteem, you know, like on the most segregated day of the week, Sunday mornings. This is evidenced by the outcomes of our endeavors, from global warming and thinning ozone to famine, earthquakes, and global anxiety. If our actions were correct, sustainable, and healthy, they would complement the already existing ecosystems of men, animals, and Mother Earth, instead of its antithesis, though, we self-reward ourselves as progressive, speaking and saying certain things but routinely behaving in a contrary fashion. Not just today or yesterday or last week or last year but even yesteryear. As mentioned above, Willie Lynch in 1712 was all but comparing notes with the ancient Romans as they used "cords of wood" to build crucifixes versus the slaveholders' use of the rope, as he clearly felt a kinship with his European brothers. Maybe he was referring to Pontius Pilate in his humiliation, torture, and then crucifixion of Christ, who, by the way, is the one they and we Christians all continue to pray to today, doesn't make sense does it, fragmented, discombobulated irrational thinking. The controlling parties during Jesus's time as well as today are closely akin. Though, certainly not all are, for there is constant pushback and confronting of their bizarre, self-serving, insensitive, selfish, non–God-fearing behavior. The Civil War and Lincoln's Republicans' (which mirrored today's Democrats) pushed to emancipate the slaves is but a healthy example of this intolerance as there are numerous efforts documented throughout history. Nevertheless, controlling groups of then and now share a common thread of little respect for those things divine—people, earth, principles, the honoring of God, for all that matters is their material wealth. Does this represent a character flaw, or a neurological defect? For it would almost have to be rooted somehow in DNA because it remains consistent over time. Connect the dots and it all comes into view. Their unbalanced and unprecedented greed, detachment, and disregard for all things divine marginalizes all else until satiety is achieved. Though it is clear satiety will never come, at least not before all things living are destroyed. This behavior is no different than that of a drug addict or thief stealing in the night. Is this a sign of strength, or weakness? Are the perpetrators of these frauds close to God, or further removed from him? Rationalizing behavior much like a cocaine addict, with a slick tongue and smooth actions for that drug is the only thing on their minds, period. No regard for family, possessions, job, health, well-being, or life—any life including their own for that matter, or God—and the list continues. This is no different. In light of all the atrocities of the past up to and including the crucifixion, and the present concerns of destroying the planet is unconscionable, yet the brakes are nowhere to be found. Listen to those that continue to push the envelope of total disregard for all things divine. They are the Willie Lynches and Pontius Pilates of the world, not to be trusted and quite frankly probably can't help themselves, needing a shot of dopamine for some spiritual revival. So from now on, when you watch them pray, just know it is not Jesus that they pray to but his nemesis.

ARCHITECTS AND DESIGNERS OF OUR WORLD

● ●

2-7-14

Preface: This next article is slightly more race sensitive, not subjective and emotional but objective, and as a matter of fact, there are events in history that are certain and clearly occurred under European watch. Careful, though, this is not a blanket indictment against all Europeans as that would be foolish and ill-informed, for it is equally as clear that whites resisted and died at the hands of those same offenders perpetrating these many frauds against humanity and mankind throughout history. They too recognized, opposed, and rejected these vile ideologies and inhumane practices as if they were too the primary targets of such unjust treatment. If those that consider the slave as the "radical," the bad guy, for attempting to escape a centuries-old institution of inhumane treatment of beatings, hangings, rape, splitting of bodies by pulling them in opposite directions by whipped horses tied to each limb, and denial of freedom, and not the system that perpetrated this fraud, then what follows more clearly defines you. Also, to those that consider Martin King a radical for attempting to improve the lives of millions of Americans and not Bull Connors, who unleashed police dogs on unarmed women and children and hosed them down with high-pressure fire-hydrant water, likewise, the following more closely defines you. But there were those whose hearts never embraced such unjust treatment and whose white skin was as much of a target and at times more of a target than those of darker pigment; they clearly are excluded from the discussion that follows, for our focus is on the spiritually ill. The first steps to solving a problem are to first admit there is one and then identify it, for only then is correction a possibility. Unfortunately, this illness still influences our daily lives, and if not corrected, we as a nation and as fellow terrestrial citizens are headed for the abyss. Follow the truth wherever it takes you. As a scientist, observing nature is an objective phenomenon. You throw a rock up, it comes down. This principle is independent of agenda or emotion. It is consistent and as old as time. It is what it is.

A neighborhood changes in five to ten years, not to mention twenty or thirty. Most readers, I'm sure, have witnessed deterioration of their own childhood domiciles and neighborhoods over such spans of time. Sure, always there are exceptions; however, deterioration and change more closely reflect the norm. Let's continue along that avenue of thought to evaluate the domiciles and neighborhoods of the world as they extend back to the dawn of man. Yet most contemporary observers will focus on the tip of the historical iceberg of mankind's razor-thin edge for their unexplored, limited, ignorant, manipulative conclusions regarding their positions reflecting the world and its people. We are dismissing true history in exchange for *his story* and inaccurately assuming that today's conditions of the planet have always been as they are since the beginning of time. Every one of us have taken part in some type of cover-up in our life span, whether simple and benign like hide-and-seek during childhood or, as an adult, intentional and malignant. Nevertheless, we all are aware of the effort and emotion. But what is consistent is our determination to conceal, manipulate, and hide, or simply, to modify the truth is directly proportional to the perceived benefit of "not being found out." Extreme in cases of great reward up to and including lying, stealing, killing, and perpetuating frauds against whatever stands before them; people, country, nature, God—it doesn't matter. And to complicate matters further, provided the initial fraud is successful, is having to continue the lie once it yields what's perceived as value. This scenario, although simple, explains and helps to delineate some of the nonsense and polluted values reinforced daily, we define as rationalization by the minds of those we consider as the establishment. They are really nothing more than dishonorable thieves seated among us. Is it true that in our society, wherever money goes favor follows; however, if we were truly spiritual and God-fearing as we attempt to portray, the script would read more like, among the spiritual, wherever truth goes favor follows.

Now reach a little further back to say fifty years and note the total absence of structures or entirely new neighborhoods. Without proper orientation, you may not even know where you are. Our world is quite the same. Following Pangaea separation, as the landmasses drifted to their respective latitudinal and longitudinal locations, climate, as a function of the earth's location in its orbit while revolving around the sun, favored specific landmasses with the appropriate conditions of moisture and temperature that created that primordial soup to which all things living owe its allegiance. The biblical Garden of Eden geographically lies in northern Africa close to the equator, with boundaries that include some configuration that includes the Euphrates and Tigris Rivers, where historical as well as biblical truths intersect, giving birth to those two famous characters Adam and Eve. For man did not appear on the earth until the earth itself, together with all its members of the whole community of living species, welcomed him to the table of symbiosis. There clearly was an alliance or treatise among all things living with Mother Earth, for it is from her womb that all things living were born and from her generosity that all things living are sustained. The mother continent, now much like that neighborhood of mankind's youth, has experienced significant strife, deterioration, and change, for there is an identifiable cause. In the chosen soil of mankind's birth, most things of value were deposited—which include natural resources from oil, diamond, gold, silver, and other precious metals to an abundance of fruits, nuts, and berries, animals of varied genomes, breathtaking views as the Garden of Eden should have, and the original man. Unfortunately, this land has been experiencing significant rape of all resources, most of which transpired at the hands of nonnatives, without any efforts of recultivation or reinvestment. As we happen upon images of mankind's place of birth, how is that experience now processed? Are there any mentions of the previous civilizations' accomplishments, as the foundation of most societies of the world, without the mental, emotional, and spiritual corruptness? Note, Egypt was performing neurosurgery, building pyramids, and mapping the star systems while the rest of the world still lived in caves. No, I'm sure much is excluded, for education would defeat the purpose or redirect the attention positively toward those and their descendents we fear and wish to continue to exploit. Connect the dots, for these conclusions are coveted by history, not the author. So futuristically, as we wield our artificial, insecure, incomplete, condescending false attitudes of superiority, I recommend that one first complete their homework. No one can save you from the truth or the wrath thereof, for currying man's favor in exchange for God's, for man has none to give as he continues the sanctioning of disobedience. Claiming manhood based on some nebulous self-defined equations—which involve the variables of bank accounts, professions, vehicles, business accomplishments, home ownership, status, deceiving, stealing, and killing, all of which lie well outside of God's wisdom—need you revisit scripture as to Jesus's possessions and posture prior to facing Pontius Pilate's wrath. God couldn't care less about those things we hold in highest esteem. All the gadgets and toys we preoccupy ourselves with are manmade distractions, kind of like those false, pagan gods of yesteryear. By the way, having a penis and testicles only defines one as a male, not a man; a man is of a different order. A man lives in his ideas, principles, and values as only God can sanction such, and the status of which cannot be bought off shelves or racks but paid for, particularly in this world with blood, sweat, and tears. For it is far more difficult to do the right thing than the wrong. Its assignment is one of honor, much too grand for the likes of most.

History leaves but a broad trail of oppression and misconduct as it relates to the treatment of other people and other creations of God's kingdom at the hands of the ruling class for some two thousand years. What characteristics encourage constant contempt for nature's order? For this is a spiritual illness, and like other illnesses, if not treated or opposed, for centuries has jeopardized our privileged existence on this planet in peril. Acknowledgment need not be given to the conditions of today, for it is pervasive and obvious even to the untrained eye. Record tornados, floods, temperature changes, and hurricanes like never seen in recorded history; record devastating earthquakes and cyclones; record wildfires, gas prices, home foreclosures, bank debacles, economic crises, and pivotal to all, extreme contempt among the nations of men. Whose decisions all but painted this wall of modern times? Is it true that a man is never truly happy until a man is truly dead? Aren't present conditions but an extension of what ails from within? We placate one another with a false sense of having correct or godly intentions that more closely resemble ungodly ones, for the proof is in the pudding. If our paths were compatible with God's wisdom, there would be no disagreements and conflicts within nature or within the hearts of men. As we claim a conscience that falls way short of threshold, not registering even neutral, it's apparent that rationalization aids us in turning a blind eye completely from God's reality. I guess it should come as no surprise, for anyone that would modify and manipulate the word of God for their financial gain is certainly an animal that cannot be reached but truly dangerous, an absolute abomination of nature.

Recognize any consistencies over the past two thousand years, from the crucifixion of Christ and enslavement of Africans, to the robbing and killing of the American Indians and gassing of the Jews? That same will now expresses itself as thinning ozone, and all that it entails, with continued social strife. The common denominator of which is European control. Consistent, repeatable, predictable, corrosive behavior to all things divine is certainly not reflective of divineness but its antithesis. The weather reports receive daily recognition for extreme temperatures, overall warmer global temperatures, excessive rainfall and flooding, unprecedented ice and snowstorms, more tornados stronger than ever recorded, tsunamis, hurricanes whose sizes and strengths are unparalleled, droughts, and unprecedented numbers and locations of earthquakes since recorded history, day in and day out, year in and year out. Congress's conservative wing's response is that it's not real; "there is no such thing as global warming." This is deliberate deception without a conscience and abuse of position and power to gain and protect their financial investments, whether directly or indirectly, and this occurs daily at the expense of the masses and/or God's creation. It is the attitudes of this bunch, or those like them, that is more closely akin to the Europeans or ruling class described above. Most are covered with filth and dishonesty, though unfazed, for corruptness pays and also accepts payment for destroying nature as apparently it is profitable. Most are completely insensitive to the impact their actions have on nature and its people. As a matter of fact, two thousand years of practice deem them professionals as they fully embrace the profitability of destroying God's kingdom with a clear conscience.

It is this flawed personality trait of greed, detachment, or lack of conscience and obvious spiritual deficiencies that are rooted at the feet of all the above-mentioned behavior that have shaped and molded our world past and present. In 2008 the Bush administration was forced by a federal judge to release documents acknowledging the effects of global warming compiled by our own government, though he unashamedly, consistently denied its existence. This action, in equivalence in the world of the practice of medicine, would be considered beyond gross negligence and deemed nearly indefensible in a court of law. This information was scheduled for release in 2004 but was suppressed until 2008. Shortly thereafter, Congress voted down a global warming bill, which would have placed some stipulations on industry in an effort to curb these adverse outcomes, and they rationalized it as "bad for business"—sounds familiar? This is where statements like "to be on the knowing end of destroying God's creation with such zest and zeal is spiritually ill" comes from. Now does this sound like God's work, or his antithesis? We too are equally guilty as our actions and selections of leadership, which continue to reflect unhealthy, narrow-minded, ungodly choices, for we somehow rationalize them with knees bent in prayer as the focus is always the nonhuman aspects or monetary in exchange for people. Now you tell me which God's preference is. Does this reflect our inner environments as well, or is this illness, like a communicable disease, contagious? If so, vitamin truth is needed to strengthen our resistance and constitution, or should I say vitamin G for God?

So as mentioned above, the abomination is so, for something has to explain this aberration in nature as it reflects obvious, deliberate, premeditated decisions of conflict, death, and destruction, consistently, again and again, all while their knees are bent in prayer. Go figure. This group represents the primary vector or source of pathology. The spread of which relies on victims of weak or weakened constitutions. This is likened to learned bad behavior for some obvious tangible benefit, be it their need to correct their own feelings of inadequacy and self-worth by currying favor and identifying with their perception of the superior culture, or maybe even perhaps financial gain. But what is clear is that it does occur as a result of some flawed rationale; it has to be flawed because the source is. As the old saying goes, it appears that they all lined up to drink the poison. Again credit the perpetrators of this social fraud, for their methods are undeniable and far-reaching, but now it's time to unravel, for all our existence depends on it. As the captain of our modern societal ship, control and navigation of our world are left at the discretion of the spiritually ill. We all must step up efforts to become good stewards and excise this cancer before it's too late.

As a trained chemist and physician, for me the study of nature is but second nature, as is recognizing the consistent, ubiquitous force within nature, which I define as God. The force is everywhere and responsible for everything and is best demonstrated on an atomic level. The atom is the smallest particle known to man and is to the physical world what the letters of the alphabet are to the English language. The combinations of which create everything physically known. The atom consists of a central mass known as the nucleus, which is comprised of protons and neutrons, and subatomic particles known as electrons, which orbit the central mass while spinning on its own axis. These internal dynamics of the atom are governed by naturally occurring forces consistent throughout nature. Next, the atoms combine with one another to create molecules, which are slightly larger structures. Again, these combinations also are governed by consistent forces in nature, specific, exact, and consistent throughout creation and time. The next step involves molecules combining with other molecules to create larger and larger particles. These combinations too are governed by the force. As the physical world slowly comes into view, none of which represents hocus-pocus but reflects the natural order throughout the universe, micro—and macrocosms. Also, it is important to note that the small, or micro, particles equal the whole as they essentially function the same. The cell of the liver functions the same way as the macro-organ that they create. Further, the functioning of our star systems and galaxies reflect the same principles of function as does its smallest part, the atom. Now follow this logic. The sun, representing the central mass, or nucleus, is orbited by the equivalent of "electrons" known as planets as they spin on their own axis while orbiting the central mass, just as in the atom. Again, this order is governed by that same force, referred to as electromagnetism on the microscale and gravitational on the macro, as it reaches throughout existence, influencing every level of interaction. Nevertheless, this established order is a by-product of the force, which is consistent, ubiquitous, controlling, equilibrated, and responsible for all. That force is God.

Now one step further, as we are all aware, certain disease processes have a predilection for one race or another. For example, hypertension, stroke, and prostate cancer are much higher in blacks than other races. By the same token, to name a few, Alzheimer's, Parkinson's, cystic fibrosis, and depression occur at a higher rate in whites than other races, while diabetes and stomach cancer are higher in Hispanics and Asians, respectively. It is at this juncture I would like to turn the attention to our world and all that ails. As the "Architects and Designers of Our World", say over the past two thousand years, our direction has undeniably bent to the will of the Europeans. What role did illness play in its creation, if any? As we study the creations of an artist, the expressions of which reflect his inner environment—his thought processes, likes, dislikes, and even illness. True, today, there is much to be grateful for, but is that truly an objective opinion, as that opinion reflects only the environment that it knows, which happens to be the same one that is in focus. In other words, there is no other standard that we know, for it is impossible to yield objectivity when a standard is measured against itself. Nevertheless, history leaves behind a trail of conflicts that clearly reflects illness and inconsistencies within God's creation.

As mentioned above, what does the crucifixion of Christ, the enslavement of the Africans, the robbing and killing of the American Indians, the gassing of the Jews, and thinning ozone all have in common? They all happened under European watch. More precisely, it is an expression of the artist, the creator of such theater, as it reflects the inner environment of the European male. And no, this is not a categorical indictment, for not everyone of European descent is stained with the blood of these atrocities—just as some diseases have a predilection for certain races, not everyone will develop them—but what is clear, however, is that it did occur. As discussed above, the concept of the part equaling the whole also applies to our society. As the "Architects and Designers of Our World", the wall of modern times was painted by the will of the white male as it is the extension of his mind and nature that mirrors our world. That being said, what is it about this beast that allows, encourages, defends, and continues such ungodly actions, clearly consistent, effortless, and without a conscience, as if spiritually ablated or spiritually ill. Perhaps neuroscience may shed some light on this matter.

Although we are all the same in the eyes of God, physically, emotionally, and spiritually, there are some distinct differences. These differences mainly reflect evolutionary adaptations based on environmental circumstances. Africa provides an abundance of sun and warmth and, as a by-product, produces food and creature comforts for all. An abundance of nuts, fruits, and berries, as well as a temperate climate that encourages cooperation among all things living, the African, not unlike other races of color, has always maintained a special relationship with Mother Earth. The intensity of the sun's ultraviolet rays stimulated a physiological protective adaptation in the integument systems of these people known as melanin, as well as kinking the hair and elongating their bodies for cooling. Melanin is the protein that, among other things, produces the dark skin in people of African descent, i.e., people of the sun. The simplified biosynthetic pathway looks something like this: L-phenylalanine—> L-tyrosine—> L-dopa—> several other reactions—> melanin. This biosynthesis occurs in the melanin-producing cells of the skin known as melanocytes. L-dopa is not only a key protein in this biosynthetic pathway but also a pivotal and essential protein in the brain for the neuronal production of dopamine. Dopamine is a neurotransmitter that is synthesized in dopaminergic neurons of the brain and plays a significant role in normal healthy brain activity, namely, a portion of the cerebral cortex known as prefrontal cortex and the basal ganglion. Dopamine production in the brain looks something like this: L-phenylalanine—> L-tyrosine—> L-dopa—> dopamine—> norepinephrine—> epinephrine (adrenaline). Glossing over, in the brain, dopamine plays a role in motor control, motivation, arousal, cognition, and reward. The basal ganglion is responsible for the execution of smooth, coordinated, refined muscle movements. In fact, I'm sure most people are familiar with Parkinson's disease as it represents deficiencies of dopamine in the basal ganglion. Clinical signs and symptoms may include tremor, slowed movement, rigid muscles, impaired posture and balance, loss of automatic movements, and speech changes. However, compromised execution of smooth, coordinated, refined muscle movements at steady state can be observed when simple refined tasks are performed, such as dancing. The prefrontal cortex is in charge of abstract thinking and thought analysis. It is also responsible for regulating behavior. This includes mediating conflicting thoughts, making choices between right and wrong, and predicting the probable outcomes of these actions. Since the prefrontal cortex is responsible for taking in data through the body's senses and deciding on actions, it is most strongly implicated in human qualities like consciousness, general intelligence, personality, and humans' ability to feel guilt. A damaged prefrontal cortex can negatively impact a person's ability to assess situations or perform tasks, particularly those of a moral or ethical nature. In short, it is at this level of neural processing that spiritual awareness and presence exist and probably can be safely labeled as the spiritual center of the brain.

Now, on the flip side, environmental factors impacting the evolution of the European are a different set of circumstances. However, they too experienced environmental pressures to adapt so as to ensure their survival in a cold, sunless, hostile environment. Just as the ultraviolet radiation from the sun impacted the African in the direction of elaborating melanin production as a protective mechanism, the lack of sunlight and heat in the hills of Europe suppressed this adaptation in people of European descent, which yielded lighter skin and straight hair. Also physical adaptations occurred to the body habitus by rounding the trunk so as to preserve heat in the central core and developing shorter, more powerful legs, used for navigating the tough terrain and hill climbing in central Europe. Food, unlike in Africa, was quite scarce as was heat and other creature comforts, until the discovery of fire. Nevertheless, basic survival was extremely challenging on a day-to-day basis and over time, by necessity, generated a much more aggressive, hardened animal. In fact, due to the cold, sunless environment, agricultural yields of nuts, fruits, and berries were limited. It is at this juncture that meat became a staple in the European diet, for meat provided much higher calories in smaller portions when compared to fruits, nuts, and berries. This is also an evolutionary pressure that encouraged elaboration of tools for hunting and later for battle between rival clans. These pressures of survival shaped the Europeans' attitudes regarding battle and war early on in their evolutionary chain, whereas in Africa, because of the abundance of food and a year-round comfortable climate, Africans casually lived under such evolutionary pressures to elaborate such weapons to hunt or the same mentality for battle and war.

I would like to now bring our focus to this obvious difference in color as an environmental adaptation, which also has other far-reaching implications. The machinery of melanin production in Africans and their descendants is much more active than in Europeans. I suppose this is obvious. So the biosynthesis L-phenylalanine—> L-tyrosine—> L-dopa—> several other reactions—> melanin is much more prevalent in the skin of people of color as are these concentrations of proteins needed for the melanin-producing machinery. As discussed above, L-dopa is a pivotal protein in the production of both melanin and dopamine. We also know from the previous discussions what psychological processes and physical activities are controlled by dopaminergic neurons or dopamine producing cells in the brain. However, our focus at this juncture is the prefrontal cortex as it is responsible for the consciousness, the ability to or not to feel guilt, and the moral or ethical processing area I define as the spiritual center of the brain. As demonstrated in other dopaminergic neurons of the brain, these neurons' ability to function optimally is directly proportionate to the availability of the neurotransmitter dopamine. The more dopamine, the higher the function, and likewise, the lesser the dopamine, the lesser the function. This concept and phenomenon is paramount to further discussion and perhaps sheds some light into the modern history of man. It is the mind and decisions of the European male that has shaped, molded, and painted the walls of modern times, and remember, the part equals the whole. This mind is the smallest cell of the value system of our society as it extends projections responsible for the creation of our social fabric. So it is this state of mind and being we wish to explore, for history is but a symptom of what ails from within. This state of mind is obviously a product of evolution as it relates to the development of aggression as a necessary character trait of survival in the hills of Europe. The cold, hostile environment challenged life at every turn. The evolutionary pressures for survival created the elaboration of tools for hunting that doubled as instruments of battle and war, taking on a mentality and direction of its own. What hasn't been discussed is the sun's ultraviolet radiation or lack of the sun's ultraviolet radiation affecting the integument system, or skin, of the Europeans and ultimately their nervous system.

As discussed above, the author has postulated that some aberration in nature contributed and contributes to the flawed actions of the Europeans' handling of God's kingdom over the past two thousand years, for that is a given, much like the answer at the back of the math book that you work back from when attempting to solve a difficult question. The author theorizes this reflects some type of spiritual illness, not in a deragatory sense but as a matter of fact . The mechanism of which is surmised to be rooted in the underperformance of the prefrontal cortex. This is a dopamine-driven area of the brain, that needs adequate availability of substrate, or dopamine, to function properly. Lower levels yield suboptimum performance while higher levels yield optimum performance. Dopamine deficiency in the prefrontal cortex would compromise the consciousness, the ability to or not to feel guilt, and the processing of moral and ethical judgment calls. In short, dopamine deficiencies of the prefrontal cortex would compromise the spiritual center of the brain. Because people of color have the machinery to produce melanin, they have an alternative reservoir in which to draw L-dopa from, provided the brain's machinery of producing dopamine slows or dies. It stands to reason and as history has demonstrated, some but not all Europeans' brains' dopamine-producing machinery lags behind that of people of color, for clearly, only a spiritually ill group could perpetrate such ungodly acts. This also correlates with a higher incidence of Parkinson's disease in whites, as well as a higher incidence of depression. I use depression as an example because lower brain norepinephrine levels correlate with depression. And since dopamine is needed to produce norepinephrine (L-dopa—> dopamine—> norepinephrine), lower dopamine levels yield lower norepinephrine levels, and hence, a higher incidence of depression in whites. Nevertheless, underperformance of the prefrontal cortex as it relates to suboptimal dopamine levels in the brain of those with less-pigmented skin predisposes this population to insensitivity and spiritually anemic behavior toward God and his kingdom over the past two thousand years. This character trait, coupled with learned aggression, truly makes this animal one to be reckoned with. For it is this aberration, deciding and contributing to decisions, that will affect our futures and our planet's future, as the boundaries of their decisions extend far beyond biblical, spiritual, and sensible lines. The above-defined ails, which I think most will agree are ails, can only be perpetrated and rationalized by one of little to no conscience, that feels little to no guilt and/or struggles with moral and ethical questions. Again, now what does the crucifixion of Christ, the enslavement of Africans, the robbing and killing of the American Indians, the gassing of the Jews, and the thinning ozone with continued social strife have in common? These frauds against humanity and God's kingdom were and are perpetrated by those with suboptimal-performing prefrontal cortexes or the spiritually ill.

SOFT SPACE

· ·

(January 8, 2014)

    Flying high above the clouds west to the sunset. The headphones setting a stage by painting a reality colored with soft voices of a glowing harmony over acoustic strings and an upright base. You find yourself with incredible vision, self-awareness, and forethought as the sun crowns the mountaintops and emits a clumsy orange hue layered in all directions with powder blue. My heart kissed by these heavens sheds a tear for such beautifully scripted theater only he can do.

The Goose Had Me a Little Loose

(January 5, 2014)

While chillin' the other night, sipping libation from my favorite vessel and of course listening to those tunes, on the menu this night was old school. Let me qualify that further. *Old school* means different times to different ages. Tonight, those soulful '70s—yeah, that crowd. All the sharp edges retired, now relaxed into that state of mind that at least for the next three to four hours "I'm responsible to no one or nothing, don't have to get up in the morning, I'm chillin'," so "let that goose loose." I'm sure you all can identify with that pause to refuel—great for mental hygiene. This night I'm spending with my folks that are gone but *never* forgotten, as we exchange "Hellos" and "I miss yous." We all had a ball just chillin', awaiting the next batch of quail and perch from the old black iron skillet while the goose was loose—now there's a treat. You see, back in the day while in high school, a couple of my close buddies and I had this thing about the brain and how it worked, which we didn't have a freaking clue about, but it sure sounded good. Discussions ranged from "We only use ten percent of our brains" and what man could be capable of if he used more, to using the power of hypnosis to recall specific details such as license plate numbers and other details at crime scenes to assist in solving murder mysteries and so on and so forth. But one concept I embraced was the notion of stimulating different parts of the brain to recreate, remember, and relive different experiences. Of course, all of which was theoretical but sounded really good. Throughout my professional studies, however, still, I have yet to identify officially this as a specific science or discipline of study. But what I have come to realize and know that does approach this concept and in some ways even exceeds the expected is music. What a beautiful instrument of nature, recreating times now past though very alive, rekindling and collecting the collage of emotions from blue to red and holding them still until identified and labeled, "This was when" and "This was then." Music is the painter of your reality that is cataloged and archived in your heart and mind forever. So this night we did the early '70s, one after another, as we visited and caught up, everyone smiling as a gesture of unconditional approval and love for those times we shared and even more for the times we continue to share. Everyone was at peace, pleasant and truly enjoyed the fellowship. What a beautiful evening. We now had all refueled, drawn strength from one another, and began planning our next outing. Slowly thereafter, with full hearts and stomachs to match, the room began to empty slowly, one after another while exchanging niceties as we all eagerly await our next evening together. My dad was the last to leave and, like all dads, had to leave his son with something and said, "Although I know that goose is loose, son, but next time please remember my Jack Black."

SUCCESS MEANS DIFFERENT THINGS TO DIFFERENT PEOPLE, NO?

• •

(January 9, 2014)

Success means different things to different people. To be born with a silver spoon in your mouth—as ex–Texas governor Ann Richards so eloquently stated about former President George H. W. Bush years back while seeking reelection—is but one side of the coin, as he was wealthy at birth. He and those like him represent but one extreme. Believe it or not, they too wrestle with the burden of self-fulfillment and feelings of accomplishment. To be born into wealth doesn't define success for the child but the parents as the child remains burdened to make his own mark.

Success means different things to different people. To be born without a silver spoon in your mouth more closely reflects the masses, and even it is multilayered, for the points of origin vary greatly. Some adults are challenged just providing the basic necessities for themselves; others are challenged providing basic necessities for their families as their twinkle is unmatched. Nevertheless, the bar is raised to range from staying out of jail and attending college, to getting a job and marrying, as the possibilities are endless and equally as varied.

Nevertheless, success is but one in the eyes of God, for he is the equalizer. No soul is valued more or less than the other. Above, the ways and means are measured against creations of choice, below, no. The bar is equal for all, fair, possible, and expected, as its focus is the true sweet spot, that spiritual bull's eye, for spiritual success is the goal as the varied numerators are balanced by a common denominator, his number; the constant, that reminds us so.

THE BEAST

• •

(December 23, 2013)

The beast is an honored and honorable being. He sprouts from the humblest of circumstances, never knowing his plight or abilities until circumstances permit, arousing the fire within. Foreign to him as well are layers of instinct and aggressions coupled with a special kindness that is devoted to obedience beneath the stormy sky. An unusual willingness to sacrifice self for principle and truth, without choice or reluctance. Skilled, gifted, and flawed, he struggles through life in a manner defined by most as reckless, though, self-directed with purpose, the purpose of service to the order in all its splendor. Oddly enough, though, however expected, the grain of society creates wear and tear far too often. It manages to stand in the way to compete alternatively and opposite for his loyalty, but not to no avail. Nourish the beast and witness its vulnerability as it purrs. Marvel at its kindness as it moves in all directions like soft ripples expanding from a central splash in a country pond beneath a beautiful, crisp, clear spring sky. Nourish the beast for as a soldier he's never discharged from duty even as he struggles to his feet only to be left alone standing in a pool of his own blood.

Mate of the Beast

· ·

(December 23, 2013)

When the beast chooses a mate, not just any will do; a "soldierist," if such a word exists, is needed to mirror, understand, and respect his plight as one of many chosen for such a fight. Hollowness is not allowed; substance and fortitude is required as her plight too is but a winding road of many sharp turns, overlooking angles with sharp descents. Defined as unconventional by the contemporary norm that's seated outside of the first that embraced the sun at its dawn and inhaled His breath even as her rib glistened in the early morning garden mist . She vowed to always remain obedient and devoted to the beast without exception, for as he bleeds, as soldiers so often do, her vessels will readily empty to fuel his plight. For his life belongs to her, as well as all, as he fights to exercise his will as is carved on the tablets of stone.

Comfort Is Yet to Come

· ·

As I listen to the tunes of my life, particularly at the corner of calm and tranquil times, the sax indelibly sketches images of love, peace, and dreams of bright yet trying futures for us all. We struggle to find the womb of comfort in a world not fully understood without recognizing the flip-side message so apparent. Comfort is yet to come, for hell is for purification; only then does the all await.

THE TRUTH NEVER HIDES, WE DO

I've waited for this moment most of my life to express and delicately couch the words to convey meaning as it has occurred and was revealed. Never a secret and always before us, the truth never hides. The teacher has always provided the path our challenge is to follow.

INTERSECTION

Chill with me. Truly feel the texture of my mind and the fabric of my soul. Come with me to the intersections of my life and humble yourself as to its meanings. Allow yourself to marvel at the truths that God has placed before us. It takes wisdom and strength to embrace that that is greater than yourself. For if that zenith is to be reached, this is the path we all must follow.

Her Heart Has No Hope

• •

A woman once said, "I don't dig that about you." My question is, Why? Created in the image of our Maker, mentally, emotionally, and spiritually, I was a bit taken aback. For the beauty of this woman was defined by the ages as vulnerable as she was beautiful, the embodiment of the rib as it glistened in the presence of her Maker. Yet she was shy from the responsibility to belong to, that lived within her. As time unfolded, it became very clear her reservation. Time and time again her yearning for the truth ended in dismay, and now her heart has no hope, only cynicism masquerading as aloofness.

College poetry, Fisk University

• •

published in the Fisk Herald,

fall of '78 through spring of '80

Enhancement, interpreting, and understanding life intrigues me immensely. Hours upon hours of my time are occupied deliberating in an effort to bridge the apparent unbridgeable gulf that separates man from the secrets of life. Concurrent with my thoughts and ideas, I detect social as well as mental blocks, occurring in the forms of shallowness and unthoughtfulness; that restricts the zenith of life-happiness. Through many of my literary work, cognitive suggestions are posed as an instrument to remedy social problems and to create a realistic, internal serenity.

A mystical voyage that recedes into the epitome of my deepest thoughts. Existing life is a question capable of staggering an entire population, although theories are presented to explain such phenomena. Life is a mystical voyage that recedes into the epitome of my most intense thoughts. (Fall 1978)

UNIQUENESS, THAT'S ALL

· ·

(Fall 1979)

There is no being on the planet

Greater than yourself

Nor are you greater than

Anyone else

We differ only by virtue of our

Unique qualities

Expansions

· ·

(Spring 1978)

The earth is the cradle of mankind,

But one cannot live in the cradle forever.

Time

· ·

(Spring 1978)

The present performs as an intimate hinge

Between an indefinite past and an indefinite,

Undefined future—the present.

CONSIDER

• •

(Fall 1978)

To accompany all adversities, there is a seed of

Greater benefit—it will not be revealed unless searched for.

DO NOT DEMAND

• •

(Spring 1978)

We should not always look with disapproval upon those who are different from us.

Little do we know they may be capable of great inventions. Do not demand absolute

conformity.

Look Up

. . . .

(November 1978)

Look up, look up, and recognize the sequined beauty of a cold and crisp night.

Appearing so vast, so modest and serene, but facilitates the remarkable potential of

linking man with the secrets of the universe.

Starlit skies, expressed by great distance and much mysticism.

It sometimes displeases me, for individuals to ignore the puzzling but innate capacity

of interstellar space.

Look up, look up, and as I do, I perceive an endless horizon that promises an unsure

future but holds the key to my tranquility.

Recognize the sequined beauty of a cold and crisp night.

I Am You

· ·

(February 1979)

I am you.
I am your mind.
Though I am a bit disappointed.
Many of you detrimentally neglect me,
Misplace and hide me in the cold, dark basement of your id.
Without recognizing my innate characteristics;
I am the industry of thought,
The vehicle of consciousness,
The emotion of love, happiness, and joy,
The interpreter of your every encounter.
Moreover, I am the uniqueness of your very being.
Please allow me to flower, even though my bloom may differ in color, size, and texture.
Let me grow, for it is intrinsic.
Let me breathe and reflect upon the world that which
I really am.
Do not be afraid,
For I am you.
. . . I am your mind.

Plateau of Life

(Spring 1979)

As perpetual as time, as uncertain as the future, the plateau of life is forever being altered.

Introspection

(Fall 1978)

In order to achieve success in life, you will first have to develop a confident and stable mental attitude. And after successfully attaching these two dimensions to your mental body, all that is performed will be an advancement.

I Sincerely Think So

(Fall 1978)

I sincerely think so. It's truly a delightful experience to be acknowledged as an individual and not just as an image of optical impression. People of shallow and simple thoughts will often evaluate a person as a result of visually observing their physical possessions or characteristics, while the most significant characteristic is voided—the mental train of thought. Ultimately, human beings are stripped of their compiled individualism and merely appear as an illusion; a resolution is to experience the spiritual aspects of life, and then you may say with confidence, "My character has improved . . . I sincerely think so."

LIFE

(Fall 1978)

Life is a vast horizon, which comprises the morning hue.

Life is a realm of intriguing questions with no apparent answers.

Life is love and if it is abused.

Life is a tunnel of darkness with no inlet of light.

Life is ambition and when openheartedly accepted.

Life is beautiful.

Life is similar to time in that if it is unwisely used.

Life is lost.

Life is the perpetual surge for survival.

Life is you.

Life is me.

Life is us.

Life is . . .

CHANGE

· ·

(Spring 1979)

Gradually life changes in form and in acquaintance. One will seldom despair for what he does know but for what he doesn't know.

THE ANTHONY

· ·

(Spring 1979)

And after seeing the great lights at darkened times and experiencing Within myself what no other has, I am no longer just a human being . . . but an individual.

THERE'S ME

• •

(Spring 1979)

There are oppressive leaders and innocent bleeders.

There are pompous aristocrats and intriguing diplomats.

There are prominent scholars and devout followers.

There are national aggressors and city professors.

There's me.

The Light

•••••••••••••••••••••••••••••••••

(September 28, 1980)

We exist as pawns of creation to be shifted and altered as the Creator allows. however,

careful deliberation and strategy govern his respected moves in this game-life. excited

to a state of confusion and unhappiness, we tend to contest the validity of his moves.

without recognizing the potential insight it provides. all things happen in search of

higher meaning it's only dark, because our eyes are closed to the light.

Untitled

•••••••••••••••••••••••••••••••

(6-83)

. . . a life untouched by feelings, and yes, suffering, is a life absent of growth.

WARRIORS

(Fall 1980) nations are at war, near and far, though, within principles, values, and understanding are captured, taken as hostages into the land of waste and mimic, reflective of you listen for the cries from within, which stem from loneliness, insecurity, shallowness and unhappiness—"HELP," and respond respond as a warrior, brave and tall, feel no fear, ... for it is the enemy trust yourself, ... for it is the armor rely on the compass of your mind to direct you into the land of waste and mimic to, in effect, conquer yourself follow this path to success, despite the pestilent mountains, darkened valleys, highways, and by ways of your mind maintain hope and refuse to grow tired, for you are a warrior fighting for a just cause—freedom even before you're consciously aware—you are a victor an all-time warrior capable of once again weaving within yourself the fiber of these conquered treasures

He who conquers himself is the greatest warrior.

THE IGNORANCE OF SOCIETY

● ●

(Fall '78)

Without limits or concern, the ignorance of society is like a cancer; it grows sickens

and pains until eventually it kills.

PUPPETS

● ●

Tenaciously, I lasted long enough to reflect true essence of composite existence. i

knew life well enough to realize that it is i, and I alone who may sincerely avouch for

my life expectancies and desires. i alone, am capable of peering through the windows

of cognition and seeing that which fascinates and intrigues me, maintaining the gist

of mental existence. if external sources are successful in distorting my interests, by

virtue of introducing fragments from their inner visions, I will no longer wield the

innate capacities of self-desire and discipline, though. i will remain to dangle as a

puppet on the string.

Your Gifts

· ·

(December 2013)

We find it easy to point out with undoubting accuracy the talents and gifts of others,

but we can never identify our own.

BIOGRAPHY

• •

I was born Anthony Kirk Williams in Marshall, Texas, to Laura Veazey and Alphonza Williams. Five years later, my baby brother, Alford Lloyd Williams, was born prematurely and died shortly thereafter. Nevertheless, I have always taken him with me. I attended Marshall Public School before graduating magna cum laude with a BS degree in chemistry from Fisk University in Nashville, Tennessee. I was awarded a medical degree from Baylor College of Medicine in Houston, Texas, and began practicing emergency medicine after training in surgery at Baylor Affiliated Hospitals. I now have over twenty-five years of experience. I am the proud father of four boys whom I refer to as my young Einsteins—truly exceptional, but like all, when it comes easy, it's taken for granted. I often have to remind them where their sharp minds for music, math, biology, chemistry, and physics come from, jokingly of course, because the truth be known, they blow me away. How appropriate as the old saying goes, "Behold the only thing greater than yourself." Collectively, they have and are studying at Baylor College of Medicine, Rice University, Northeastern University, Harvard University, Carnegie Mellon University, St. Thomas University, Lamar University, and Morehouse College.

Through many of my literary works, I attempt to empower the soul of men by bringing focus to untold, purposefully omitted, naked, raw, unexpected, and often unpopular perspectives I define as truth. The truth is but a compass that surrenders to the science of the earth, bigger than us all. It aligns with our Maker's will, pointing the way. Our challenge is to follow, and that doesn't mean at our convenience or only if our comfort zone permits—it is *period*. The complexity and depth of manipulation is so commonplace that unraveling is but a near impossibility, as the will of man and God often collide. Must I remind you, this is His world, not ours. However, as you throw a rock up, it comes down. Since the beginning of time, this principle has existed, unadulterated, unmanipulated, consistent, and old as time. Mentally, emotionally, and spiritually, this same principle exists. Find it, dust it off, and use it daily as your point of reference. Peace.